COMMIES

A Journey Through
the Old Left, the New Left
and the Leftover Left

RONALD RADOSH

ENCOUNTER BOOKS
SAN FRANCISCO

First edition published in 2001 by Encounter Books, an activity of Encounter for Culture and Education, Inc., a nonprofit tax exempt corporation.

Encounter Books website address: www.encounterbooks.com

Cover and text design © Ayelet Maida, A/M Studios.
Cover image source photo from PhotoDisc.
Photographs courtesy of the author, unless otherwise indicated.

Manufactured in the United States and printed on acid-free paper.
The paper used in this publication meets the minimum requirements of ANSI/NISO Z39.48-1992 (R 1997) (Permanence of Paper).

Library of Congress Cataloging-in-Publication Data
Radosh, Ronald.
    Commies : a journey through the old left, the new left and the leftover left / Ronald Radosh.
        p. cm.
    Includes index.
    ISBN 1-893554-05-8 (alk. paper)
1. Radosh, Ronald. 2. Communists—United States. 3. Communism—United States. 4. New Left—United States. 5. Right and left (Political science). I. Title.

    HX86.R25 2001
    973'.088'33521—dc21
    2001023668

10 9 8 7 6 5 4 3 2 1

★

For Allis, with whom I share a wonderful life,
and for her love and warmth and support.

And for Laura, Daniel and Michael,
so they know where their dad is coming from.

Contents

Red Diapers

RON KOVIC, THE RADICAL VIETNAM VET, CLAIMS SARCASTICALLY to have been born on the Fourth of July; I have always thought of myself—with growing irony—as having been born on the First of May. In a sense, the first step of my journey to America, a country where I was born but didn't fully discover until middle age, took place on May Day 1939. One of the photographs I have inherited shows me as a baby, one and a half years old, bundled in a stroller and about to be paraded down Fifth Avenue in the yearly Communist Party celebration that went through the garment center of the then radical needle trade unions, ending with a mass rally at Union Square—for decades the historic center of radical protest. That day, it seems to me, was my baptism into the world of Jewish radicalism, a world so small and insular that it existed inside a political and social ghetto. It is now a lost world, yet one well captured by the late Irving Howe in his classic book *The World of Our Fathers.*

I almost didn't enter that world at all. Those in charge of preparing for "the revolution" could not afford the frivolity of having children. And when my mother found in her late thirties that she was pregnant, it was an unexpected, and in some sense an alien event. My father had come from a large family and I had many cousins; but among their friends in "the movement," my parents were almost the only ones to have a child. Politics notwithstanding, they were devoted and loving parents who continually sought my best interests, which sometimes meant shielding me from the movement's dark side.

My father, Reuben Radosh, was a milliner, having learned to design women's hats in turn-of-the-century Poland. Coming to the United States shortly before the outbreak of World War I, he was drafted into the U.S. Navy. After serving his stint, he quickly got a job at a millinery factory, where he became active in the hatters' union, officially known as the Hat, Cap and Millinery Workers of America, an American Federation of Labor craft affiliate. In that union, he became an activist in the radical caucus and served as a leader in one of the earliest Communist fronts, the Trade Union Unity League. The TUUL was an instrument set up by the Communist Party during the so-called "Third Period," when the Communist line spoke of imminent revolution and the party sought to move working-class militants out of the regular AFL unions and into a new, revolutionary trade union federation.

My father quickly became the TUUL's classic front man: a non-Communist who accepted party leadership, and who sought to get his fellow workers to split their union and move it under party control. He almost succeeded. The official history of the union, published in the 1960s, notes that in the late1920s he ran for president of the union with one opponent, the moderate trade unionist Alex Rose. My father was more radical—and also more naïve. Ballots were supposed to be listed alphabetically. But before they were printed, Rose asked my father if it would be all right for him to put his name on the ballot first. Certain that he was going to win, my father immediately agreed. He didn't realize that in the community of immigrant workers, many who still could not read English voted for the first name they saw. And so my father's magnanimity led to his electoral loss, and to a lifetime of hard work in the city's hat factories instead of a desk job among the union bosses.

Rose fared much better. Those who grew up in New York City would later all know his name. A major power broker in Democratic Party circles, Rose broke up the third-ticket American Labor Party, which had become another front of the Communists at the onset of the Cold War, and he moved labor leaders who had created it a decade earlier out of its ranks and into a new body he created, the Liberal Party.

By the time of the Cold War, my father found that his past activity with the Reds had put him on the industry blacklist.

Despite his reputation as a first-rate designer, firms were reluctant to hire him. He then did what scores of other blacklisted union activists close to the Communist Party did: he became a capitalist. He went into business with an old neighborhood friend whose cousin had owned one of the major hat firms in America. And in one of those strange quirks of history, my pro-Communist father ended up getting the contract for the official Eisenhower hats in the 1952 campaign, which he designed and which were created in the factory he now owned.

If such an event could happen only in America, the same was true of its sequel. By the 1960s, as fashion changed and few women wore hats, the industry declined and my father's firm, along with scores of others, went out of business. Alex Rose, whose strong anticommunism had long since moved him out of my father's circles, came to his rescue. Rose worked the books, allowing my father to obtain a union pension, although he had not worked as a union member for decades. It was, my father thought, Rose's way of thanking him for his naïve generosity so many years ago when he foolishly agreed to let his rival be listed first on the union electoral ticket.

My mother, Ida Radosh, née Kreichman, came from Russia with her family at an early age and lived with her parents and sister and brothers in a one-room apartment in the swarming ghetto of the Lower East Side. In those days, few of her friends or family went past elementary school, and like so many other immigrant children, she had to leave school after the eighth grade to find a job. In 1913, at the age of thirteen, she transferred to the Hebrew Technical School for Girls, to be trained in techniques of factory work in the garment trades. There she learned how to be a cutter, a task left for female workers to perform, while the men got the machine jobs. At the age of twenty-three, after spending nearly half of her days working, my mother had the major experience of her young life when she got an opportunity to attend the Bryn Mawr summer school for working women. At this union-sponsored educational session on the campus of the elite institution, she finally got a sampling of education, taking courses in philosophy, history and science; and she had a chance to swim and play tennis. In later years, she would proudly show me the one term paper she ever wrote, an essay on anarchism.

It was in the garment trades, as a member of her local's executive board in the fledgling International Ladies' Garment Workers' Union led by David Dubinsky, that Ida Kreichman met my father. Their relationship was born in the meetings that surrounded major strikes in the 1920s. My father, who had participated in the 1924 general strike of millinery workers, was by then a prominent left-wing union activist. He and my mother were clearly made for each other. At the time they both lived in Williamsburgh, then a Jewish outpost of Brooklyn. Finding themselves at the same union meeting, they walked home together over the Brooklyn Bridge. Like so many other couples involved in the trade union and radical movements, their romance was framed by life and struggle in the movement.

My parents may have thought of themselves as working-class heroes, but for me the romantic figure in the family was my mother's cousin Jacob Abrams, a charismatic, handsome young militant in the Jewish anarchist movement in New York. By the time I was born, Abrams was living with his wife, Mary, in Mexico City, a haven for exiled revolutionaries from all over the world. We visited him there many times during my childhood. Abrams (we always called him by his last name) had made a bid for fame as a radical back on August 23, 1918, when he was arrested along with four of his comrades for distributing two leaflets protesting the American intervention in the fledgling Soviet Union, the so-called Siberian Expedition of 1918. By today's lights, the leaflet reads as if it came from another planet. It accused the United States government of generating "false, hypocritic [sic] military propaganda" and betraying the workers of Germany and Russia. The only response to the expedition, which aimed to "betray the splendid fighters of Russia," was to proclaim a general strike.

The leaflets, printed in Yiddish and broken English, and handed out on a single block in New York City, would hardly appear to threaten the nation's security. Yet Abrams and his comrades were arrested by the New York Bomb Squad, and after a trial that drew a great deal of attention, were found guilty of violating the Sedition Act of 1918, which forbade inflammatory antigovernment speech. They were handed twenty-year sentences for their crime. The Supreme Court upheld the conviction, but the case led to the single most important dissent issued by Justice Oliver Wendell Holmes, one that has become the basis of all subsequent First Amendment theory and litigation.

Justice Holmes argued that Congress "certainly cannot forbid all effort to change the mind of the country." Maintaining that even during war "the principle of the right to free speech is always the same," he concluded that only "the present danger of immediate evil," or a desire to bring such about, warranted restrictions on speech. "Now nobody can suppose that the surreptitious publishing of a silly leaflet by an unknown man," Holmes wrote of my cousin, "without more, would present any immediate danger that its opinions would hinder the success of the Government arms or have any appreciable tendency to do so." The prison terms, he argued, had "been imposed for the publishing of two leaflets that I believe the defendants had as much right to publish as the Government has to publish the Constitution of the United States now vainly invoked by them." What Holmes defended was not sympathy for their views, which he found silly and deplorable, but rather the "free trade in ideas" by which views get accepted or rejected in "the competition of the market." Thus, he concluded in much-quoted words, "we should be eternally vigilant against attempts to check the expression of opinions we loathe and believe to be fraught with death, unless they so imminently threatened immediate interference with the lawful and pressing purposes of the law that an immediate check is required to save the country."

But that was the dissenting opinion; so Abrams began serving his sentence in a federal facility in Atlanta. After almost two years, the defendants were offered a commutation of their sentences, on condition that "they be deported to Russia and never return to the United States, or to require them to serve the sentences imposed." Thus, in June of 1922, Abrams and his wife sailed off to the still young revolutionary republic, the Soviet Union. But he quickly discovered that even then, the USSR was utopia lost.

As the scholar of anarchism Paul Avrich has written, "by the Spring of 1918, the majority of anarchists had been sufficiently disillusioned with Lenin to seek a complete break, while the Bolsheviks, for their part, had begun to contemplate the suppression of their former allies, who had outlived their usefulness and so, from the start, the anarchists found themselves the first victims of the new secret police whose incessant criticisms were a nuisance the new regime no longer had to tolerate."

Any ties left between the anarchists and the Bolsheviks came to an end after the famed suppression by Trotsky's troops of the sailors' and workers' rebellion at Kronstadt in March of 1921. Emma Goldman, who had already left Russia by the time Abrams arrived, wrote to his counsel, "we missed your young clients who I fear will not be very grateful for having been taken out of Atlanta ... and sent to the Russian Penitentiary." Indeed, Abrams soon found that one of his codefendants who had joined him in the Russian exile, Mollie Steimer, had been arrested for "anarchist" activity by the GPU, the first incarnation of the KGB. Steimer was to write that the Bolsheviks had become "the most reactionary, most brutal and autocratic rulers, who care for nothing but the maintenance of their power." The censorship, secret police and concentration camps exceeded anything that existed in the supposedly brutal United States. Russia, she put it, was "a great prison where every individual who is known not to be in full agreement with the Communists is spied upon and booked by the GPU as an enemy of the government." It was no surprise that Abrams and his wife left Russia for Paris in November of 1925, and then continued on to Mexico, whose government was known to grant political refugees a safe haven.

Despite Abrams' disillusioning experience, my parents decided to undertake the arduous trip to the USSR to check out utopia for themselves. They arrived in Paris and boarded the train, stopping in Berlin and Warsaw, and after many appeals, received a visa and were on their way. A reading of their joint diary of the trip suggests that they were taken in by the propaganda of the Leninist regime. My mother's entry for August 24, 1924, describes a spectacle of youth marching in parade at Red Square. Seven thousand children demonstrated techniques in what my mother called the work of "physical culturists," and she remarked that the children "look well taken care of, all developing beautifully." After watching the marching and listening to the bands, she commented that it was "thrilling to see the enthusiasm of the participants; they marched off the square singing joyously all new revolutionary songs." The most wonderful thing Russia is doing "is for her children."

My parents stayed at the famous Lux Hotel, the main base camp for visiting revolutionaries. One day they went to visit the exiled IWW leader "Big Bill" Haywood, who had fled to Russia to avoid imprisonment in the United States and who was a showpiece for revolutionary solidarity. They spoke with him in his room for over an hour, but unfortunately their diary reveals little of what Haywood told them. Another day (August 28), they attended a graduation ceremony for Red Army officers, where they saw a play that included an attack on religion and a sketch showing "America, Italy, France and England trying to convince Soviet Russia to compromise herself and then they would recognize her." My mother remarked that the Soviet officers were "all intelligent and polite," which was "a great contrast to the soldiers ... of the old regime." Obviously, my parents' own revolutionary euphoria blinded them to the reality that Jack Abrams and his comrades had seen.

Yet it was Abrams, the anarchist, who galvanized me as a boy. My first remembrance of the many visits we made to Mexico City is from 1945, when I was nine. As others were gathering in Times Square to celebrate the end of World War II, we saw the giant parade that wound through downtown Mexico City. Abrams took me to the major sites and to children's films, willingly spending hours with me while my parents went off to experience Mexico's revolutionary culture. In a later visit, either 1949 or 1950, Abrams, who had learned from my parents that I had already begun to circulate in the orbit of New York's young Communist movement, did his best to warn me about the ethics and true nature of Stalin's regime. As we all walked through the streets of beautiful Cuernavaca (now a famous tourist resort), my parents spotted the painter David Alfaro Siqueras, one of the founders of the Mexican muralist school. The famed artist approached

Abrams to say hello, and much to my shock, Abrams refused to shake his hand and exchange greetings. "I don't talk to murderers," he shouted at Siqueras, and turned and walked away. When he had calmed down, Abrams told me about Siqueras's role in the attempted murder of Leon Trotsky at his estate in the Coyocan suburb of Mexico City, when the painter led a group of machine-gun-toting raiders in a failed effort to kill the exiled Bolshevik.

Abrams often socialized and became friends with other exiles, despite occasionally severe political differences. He was a regular guest at Trotsky's walled-in compound, where the two played chess and argued about Bolshevism. After his death, Trotsky's widow presented Abrams a set of Trotsky's favorite Mexican-made dishware as a remembrance of their solidarity and friendship—a gift which Abrams later passed on to my parents. Often in later years, I would serve cake to my Stalinist friends on these plates, and after they admired the beauty of the design and craftsmanship, I would tell them whose dishes they were eating from, and watch them turn pale.

Abrams also befriended the great painter Diego Rivera, who spent his years moving from Bolshevism to Trotskyism and back to official Soviet Communism. Despite these twists and turns, and probably because at critical moments Rivera had opposed Stalin, Abrams maintained the relationship. Once, he took me to meet the artist and watch him paint the murals—some of the last he was to create—in the Del Prado Hotel in the main part of the city. In later years, the hotel would cover the murals with curtains because of embarrassment about their anti-Catholic and revolutionary themes. Rivera gave Abrams some of his paintings, one of which Abrams gave to my parents. My mother kept it in her New York City apartment.

Strongly objecting to the very concept of private property, my parents refused for years to buy their own home. They eventually moved into what they called a "true cooperative," the ILGWU's cooperative housing project in New York's Chelsea district. When the original loan ran out in the 1980s, and many residents wanted to privatize their contract and thus have equity to pass on to their children, my mother and others of her generation voted against that option on the grounds that individuals should not profit from their own investments. And so the irony: When my mother passed the Rivera painting on to me near the end of her life, it was precisely when the market for Mexican art was heating up; so I brought it to Sotheby's auction house in New York, where it sold for a very handsome price which became the hefty down payment for the private home in which I now reside.

In the 1930s, the event that was of consuming interest for the Left was, of course, the Spanish Civil War. Indeed, I have in my library the well-worn copy of Franz Borkenau's *The Spanish Cockpit,* a gift from Abrams when I was twelve years old. "You're too young to understand this yet," he told me, "but I assure you that when you grow older, you will." His inscription reads "To Ronald: the future philosopher." But Spain was a rather sensitive topic in my parents' home, and most of the time when our family visited Abrams, a discussion of the issues raised by the civil war was avoided by mutual agreement. Anarchists like Abrams believed that the Spanish people were fighting to preserve an authentic anarchist revolution; this position was anathema to the Communists, who argued that Spain first had to win the war against Franco, fighting on behalf of a moderate Popular Front government that, while close to Moscow, would not promote revolution. My uncle Irving Keith (née Kreichman, but like so many Jewish Communists he took a new party name the better to Americanize himself) was a commissar in the Abraham Lincoln Brigade, a role he had been trained for in the famous Lenin School in Moscow; so to besmirch the Communist effort in Spain was automatically to insult his name. Thus the subject was always put aside.

"I'm really anxious to meet your son," Uncle Irving wrote to my father in one of his letters from Spain, "but that will have to wait until the war is won." I was never to meet him, however. He was killed in battle during the spring 1938 retreat. My family honored his memory, and I grew up addicted to the romance of the International Brigades. Like the actor Richard Dreyfuss, who spoke at one of their reunion conventions in the 1980s, I too considered the vets to be authentic American heroes, men whose heroism would have been recognized by a grateful nation and world if it were not for their left-wing politics.

I read my martyred uncle's letters to my mother and father. Most of them were a series of moving assurances to his own mother, sisters and brothers that there was no need to worry; he would be home safely as soon as the war against Franco resulted in the inevitable victory. But others were long political diatribes, attempts to convince his family that the Communist Popular Front policy was correct and that the philosophy of revolution advocated by the anarchists like his cousin Abrams was wrong. "The main political problem," he wrote, "is that of strengthening the unity of the working class." By that he meant the need to get the anarchists, syndicalists and socialist "irresponsibles" to join with the Spanish Communists in support of the rather moderate, nonrevolutionary goal of saving the bourgeois republic. Worse were those in the "rearguard" who opposed Communist policy and sought to "create divisions in the Popular Front." Here, my uncle Irving was obviously alluding to the supporters of the POUM, the anti-Stalinist Communists who were fraudulently condemned as "Trotskyites" by the Comintern.

These myths of the Left—to be precise, the pro-Communist Left—became part of my intellectual marrow as I was growing up in the 1940s. They were received truths, ideas to be accepted on faith among the first lessons of life.

By the time I was three years old, my parents had moved from a small Lower East Side apartment to Washington Heights, a new middle-class neighborhood populated by Eastern European Jewish immigrants and a new group of German Jews, like the parents of Henry Kissinger, who had recently fled Hitler's Germany. Many years later I found, much to my shock, that I had actually lived in the very apartment building inhabited by Ted Hall, the notorious Soviet atom-bomb spy at Los Alamos, whose role had by then been exposed through the release of the Venona files, and whose story was told by Joseph Albright and Marcia Kunstel in their book *Bombshell.* The Halls had moved out to Forest Hills in Queens just about when my parents moved in. I have wondered if they may have moved into the Hall apartment, and if

I possibly had Ted's old room. My block, West 172nd Street and Fort Washington Avenue, was also a stronghold of numerous other Communists. A few doors down we had good friends in one family where the father was a Communist functionary, a man who disappeared and went "underground" when the Communist leaders were arrested in 1948. Other friends included a well-known "progressive" lawyer, as well as others whose general orbit was that of the front groups of the American Communist Party.

The school I attended, PS 173, was a short walk from home (in those days, we students came home for lunch and returned an hour later). The school had a largely Jewish student body; other schools in Washington Heights, depending on location, were made up primarily of Italian or black students. The neighborhood had not as yet become the largely Hispanic area, of Haitian, Dominican and other Latin American recent immigrants, that it now is. Upon dismissal at 3 P.M., I often had to run home in order to avoid the small gangs of Italian high-schoolers who showed up for the purpose of beating up younger Jewish students, thus giving me a new definition of "class struggle." One school in a large system, PS 173 had yearbooks that read like a Who's Who of successful New Yorkers. My friends and fellow students included a group of people now famous in the fields of the arts, journalism and law, like my classmate Ed Kosner, now editor of the *New York Daily News;* my friend David Margulies, now a prominent actor; Esther Kartiganer, an executive producer at *60 Minutes;* her brother Joseph, now a prominent estate lawyer; Tom Baer, a former New York assistant district attorney and now a Democratic Party activist and film producer—the list could go on and on.

But while the students of PS 173 came from homes that were largely Jewish, the teachers were mainly Irish and conservative. Our parents, of course, controlled the PTA, and this meant perpetual conflict and classroom stress. A few incidents remain vividly in my mind. Because of pressure by the PTA to recognize what was then called "Negro History Week," for instance, an event recognized in those years only by residents of Harlem and by white Communists, we were asked to bring into class an account of Negro Americans who had contributed to American society's growth and culture. Back then, the only Negroes one could find in our textbooks were Booker T. Washington, George Washington Carver, and some anonymous, happy slaves who were taken advantage of during Reconstruction, when carpet-baggers used them for their own evil purposes. So when my class-mate Jake Rosen brought in a 78 rpm record of the baritone Paul Robeson, all hell broke loose

By the onset of the Cold War, Robeson's career had been cut short, as the singer squandered his early success by dedicating himself relentlessly to a vigorous defense of the Soviet Union and Joseph Stalin. In particular, his statement at a Soviet-sponsored "peace congress" in Europe, that American Negroes would not fight on their own country's side in a war between the United States and the Soviet Union, brought down the wrath of the nation upon him. The great baseball hero Jackie Robinson reluctantly appeared in public before the House Committee on Un-American Activities to let it be known that he differed strongly with Robeson, and from that point on, the singer's career was all downhill. Of course, that meant that Robeson would become an even greater hero of the Communist Left in America, who took him to their heart and proclaimed him the nation's single greatest public figure.

Jake Rosen would gain notoriety later on as the young man who, at the Communist Festival of World Youth held in Moscow in the 1950s, is seen in an unforgettable full-page photo in *Life* magazine, dipping the American flag to honor Soviet chairman Nikita Khrushchev as he passed by with the U.S. delegation at the Moscow sports arena. And even later, in the 1960s, Rosen would become a founding member and leader of the Maoist Pro-gressive Labor Party, a Marxist-Leninist sect that made the CP look like a group of tame reformists.

The Robeson incident was no doubt Jake Rosen's first polit-ical controversy. I remember Jake putting the Robeson record on a phonograph. Hearing the gigantic, booming baritone, our teacher, Agnes Driscoll, responded in awe. She praised the singing as magnificent, which it was. Who was the singer? she asked. The official report of the Communist-led New York Teacher's Union singled out the incident and reported that when Rosen identified the singer as Robeson, Driscoll "snatched the record from the player and screamed, 'that Communist in my class!'" She then told the students that "they were Communists and she knew there were others in the class, and if they didn't like it there was a plane leaving Idlewild [airport] every hour." Rosen had to report to the principal's office, whence he was sent home for the day and suspended from classes for a week. He went home in tears, propelling the PTA into action. All of us were instructed by our parents to stay home also in protest against the misconduct charge, until the school and the teacher formally apologized to Jake and called for our return.

Miss Driscoll, one of the Irish-American conservatives who had nothing but contempt for our Red parents and us, also created an incident when we had a classroom election poll in 1948, the year of the famous Dewey-Truman race. My parents, like all of the Reds and fellow travelers in the Heights, were supporting the third-party candidacy of the former vice president and secretary of commerce, Henry A. Wallace, who was running on a pro-Soviet platform under the rubric of the Progressive Party. When a good number of our class voted in the mock poll for Wallace, Miss Driscoll erupted. Wallace was a Red and a traitor, she scolded, and in our classroom we could only vote for Dewey or Truman. Miss Driscoll went on to inform us that if any of our parents were intending to vote for Wallace, we should tell them they could not and should not. I ran home for lunch crying, because I felt that Miss Driscoll had turned her anger particularly on Rosen and me.

The incident became the first cause célèbre for the newly organized Teacher's Union. In its 1950 book *Searchlight: An Exposé of New York City Schools*, the Red-led union reported on the incident:

> The Parents Association of a school in Washington Heights sent an official letter to Superintendent [of Schools William] Jansen asking him to investigate an incident in which the teacher, Miss Agnes Driscoll, had terrified her sixth grade pupils by calling them "un-American" and "Communist." The only reply they got was from an assistant ... to the effect that the letter would be "called to the Superintendent's attention." *There the matter rested.*

Nevertheless, the PTA of PS 173 managed to win some major victories. Once, I and some other of the best students won a coveted local award given to the schools by the Daughters of the American Revolution in honor of our commitment to our studies. Each of us received a formal citation and a medal, which we proudly pinned to our lapels. When I got home, my parents were in a rage. Immediately they phoned the parents of other medal winners, and a meeting was called. They explained to us that no child of theirs could accept a medal awarded by a reactionary and racist organization, which defined Americanism as 100 percent white and which had refused to allow the Negro singer Marian Anderson to perform at Constitution Hall in Washington, D.C., where she had been booked. Their protest received much local publicity, and in tears and humiliation, my friends and I had to bring our letters and medals back to be returned. The PTA had won the fight, and nothing else was heard about the awards. But soon after, we were all forced to give up our membership in the AAA Safety Patrol, the one job at school everyone aspired to. (Being on the patrol meant wearing a strap and official badge, and monitoring the halls and traffic outside the school.) I had just achieved the rank of captain and received a special blue badge, when suddenly I was called in after the DAR protest and told to surrender the badge and hence my status as a Safety Patrol officer. In spite of my conviction that my parents were politically correct, I came home from school angry at them for creating a stink about the Daughters of the American Revolution.

2

Commie Camp

THE NAME "CAMP WOODLAND FOR CHILDREN" EVOKES A BUCOLIC picture of children romping happily in fields of green, far from the brutal summer heat of the city—a picture of swimming, hiking, baseball and camaraderie in the peaceful countryside. There was some of that at Camp Woodland, but that really wasn't the point. It was created by Communists and fellow travelers so their children could be together in the protected atmosphere of Phoenicia, New York, insulated from the Red-baiting ways of places like PS 173, enjoying a pleasant setting where the ideas, values and culture of the parents could be transmitted painlessly to their Red-diaper babies.

Camp Woodland was one of the myriad alternative institutions founded by the Communist Party in its effort to construct an alternative to America. As Paul Mishler, a left-wing academic who has written the history of these camps, so aptly put it, the camp was an attempt to build "socialism in one summer." In his book *Raising Reds,* Mishler characterizes Woodland as a place that "linked an urban-based radicalism with the 'naturally' democratic traditions of rural America." But unlike other camps that were formally tied to Communist Party institutions, Woodland was nominally independent, although it drew its staff from the Communist world. Its founder and director, Norman Studer, once a Ph.D. student of John Dewey's at Columbia University, pursued the task of uniting Dewey's theories of "progressive education"—popularly described as "learning by doing"—with pro-Soviet American radicalism. The results were to be seen in the elementary school he ran during the school year, the Downtown

Community School, and at Camp Woodland during the summer.
As Studer explained:

> The camp was part of a widespread movement of reform that was
> not new in American life, but which grew to special importance
> in the late 1930s and 1940s.
> ... The democratic ethos, the ideals of the founding fathers,
> half expressed in the Constitution, but never brought to fruition
> for Blacks, Women and Trade Unionists were being proclaimed
> for all by poets, philosophers and scientists. The people who
> founded Camp Woodland believed in this new education. They
> went further than most educators and linked the liberation of
> children firmly with the new emerging culture of democracy. For
> us, the new "progressive Education" meant more than new meth-
> ods in the classroom. It meant the creation of a new personal-
> ity to fit the new kind of culture which we saw developing in
> America.

Studer's "explanation" needs some translating. First, note the
words "liberation of children." Since the 1990s we have become
used to "progressive" organizations like the Children's Defense
Fund and the theoretical musings of those who believe in "children's rights," such as the right to sue a parent. But Studer began
Woodland in 1939, and his idea was to liberate children not from
their parents but from America. As for the "new emerging culture of democracy," Studer was clearly referring to the ethos of
the Popular Front, the Communist Party's attempt to domesti-
cate itself after the disastrous, revolutionary Third Period, when
it had demanded a break with liberals and social democrats.
Since the Popular Front was nothing less than the new, American path to socialist revolution, Studer, a good Communist, saw
institutions like Woodland as the very mechanism to create what
Stalinists would call "the new socialist man." Here, in a summer
camp where the values of the Popular Front would dictate daily
experience, the new democratic personality would be molded to
fit the socialist paradise to come.

Here is how the camp's brochure stated its purpose:

> Camp Woodland is coeducational and interracial. Children learn
> the democratic way of life by actually living it. The genuine qual-
> ity of camp democracy is attested to by the comment of an old

Catskill lumberman, who exclaimed after seeing the camp in operation: "If someone had told me that there was a place where all peoples lived and worked together I wouldn't have believed it—it's just wonderful."

For years I wondered who that old lumberman could have been.

I first went to Woodland's "senior camp" with other eleven-to thirteen-year-olds; and during my college years, I returned as a counselor. In all, I attended the camp for eight or nine years. It was at Woodland that I was introduced to folk music and Pete Seeger, who visited and sang there regularly. His father-in-law, Homeri Ohta, lived on the premises and conducted morning exercises for the senior camp before breakfast. The highlight of many Sunday meetings was to have Seeger gather before the camp at the outdoor amphitheater, where he first sang what much later would become hits for the Weavers, including his version of Leadbelly's "Goodnight Irene" and "Kisses Sweeter Than Wine." The camaraderie one felt in sitting with friends and singing the beautiful words and melodies produced a belief that all would be good in the world, and that the lovely music we were creating would help us build that better world. I remember as if it were yesterday joining Pete for a sleep-out with other counselors on the mountain above camp. Seeger woke us early in the morning, singing the old holler "Wake Up Jacob," with its line "sun's abreakin', peas in the pot and hoecakes bakin'," as he proceeded to grill bacon and eggs for us on the campfire he had built.

I am convinced that much of the radicalism that Woodlanders would carry with them in later years came from the illusions they developed as a result of the weekly sing-alongs with Seeger. Songs are weapons, he often said. And during the years of the commercial top forty "Hit Parade," before rock and roll, songs were helping us to build an alternative culture mirroring the alternative politics that Seeger was trying to create during the 1948 presidential campaign, when he accompanied Henry A. Wallace throughout the country and sang wherever Wallace appeared for his new Progressive Party.

Woodland was one of a trio of the most prominent Commie camps. The most Bolshevik was Camp Wo-Chi-Ca, whose name ironically had the trappings of a commercial "Indian" camp, with bogus totem poles, color wars and traditional camp curriculum. But Wo-Chi-Ca was not Indian at all. The name came from Workers' Children's Camp! Wo-Chi-Ca named its social hall "The Paul Robeson Playhouse" in honor of the pro-Communist black singer who had become the darling of the party, and perhaps the nation's number one defender of Stalin. His son attended the camp in 1941 and 1942, and Robeson himself often appeared at and sang for the campers. Wo-Chi-Ca's 1949 yearbook records the reception: "When Paul Robeson came there was great excitement. Everyone was pushing and screaming. . . . He went in front of the Main House, and there was everybody trying to see him through the windows and doors." Robeson, it might be said, was for the Communists what Frank Sinatra was for the other America. Other leading Communists visited the camp as well, such as the artist Rockwell Kent and the famous old-timer Ella Reeve "Mother" Bloor, who had begun her years of agitation as a supporter of William Jennings Bryan in 1896.

The camp stressed the goals of the CIO and trade unionism, and listed campers' names alongside those of the unions their parents belonged to—most of course being Communist-led unions that would eventually be expelled from the CIO. The camp also took "culture" seriously; that meant no comic books at Wo-Chi-Ca. The campers solemnly recited, "We pledge ourselves to combat the influence of jokes, comic books, newspapers, radio programs that make fun of any people." During the great 1950s comic-book scare, in which a left-wing psychologist named Dr. Frederick Wertham testified before Congress on the evil effects of superhero comics, the camp's yearbook proudly reported that the campers were asked to turn in all their comics. It was important that Wo-Chi-Ca campers not be influenced by whatever patriotic attitudes they might inadvertently pick up from a pro-American superhero such as "Captain America."

The other of the three top Commie camps was Camp Kinderland, which I'm sad to say is still evidently in business, serving the children of third- and fourth-generation Red-diaper babies.

Kinderland, affiliated with the Communist Party's fraternal organization for Jewish Communists, the International Workers' Order or IWO, was meant to transmit to the children of Eastern European Jewish immigrants the legacy of the secular Jewish radical culture developed in the Old Country.

While Robeson was the favored visitor at Wo-Chi-Ca, Kinderland went all out for the widow of the Yiddish writer Sholom Aleichem, whose portraits of *shtetl* life in Poland became the basis for the musical hit *Fiddler on the Roof.* Even the Soviet Yiddish poet Itzik Feffer, who would be murdered by Stalin in the early 1950s, visited the camp. Along with modern dance classes led by Martha Graham protégé Edith Segal, a hard-core Communist who tried to blend modern dance with Marxism, the camp featured artsy personalities like future film and stage star Zero Mostel, film director Jules Dassin, and Duke Ellington's son, Mercer.

Compared to the other two explicitly Communist institutions, my own Camp Woodland seemed almost secular. Woodland did not celebrate Soviet holidays, or bring Paul Robeson or Jules Dassin to camp, or feature skits heralding the Abraham Lincoln Brigade. The staff and the counselors may have all shared those politics, but rather than indoctrinating its campers directly, Woodland was more subtle. It honored the culture of the Popular Front—a living proof, as CP leader Earl Browder proclaimed, that communism was twentieth-century Americanism. Instead of revering martyred Communist workers like Harry Sims, a coal mine organizer from the Young Communist League killed in the 1920s, the camp taught and sang about the rough pioneers who settled the Catskill mountains, where the camp was located, in earlier decades—men like a mythical Paul Bunyan–type local hero named "Boney" Quillen, who became the subject of a cantata written by our Communist composer-in-residence, Herbert Haufrecht.

Folklorist Alan Lomax had traveled through the American South with his tape recorder, helping to resurrect such famous artists as Hudie Ledbetter (Leadbelly) and McKinley Morganfield (Muddy Waters). Camp Woodland's director, Norman Studer, tried to do the same thing, hauling his old reel-to-reel, first-generation recording machine throughout the Catskills, where he found and recorded the stories and songs of the aging singers and storytellers, all farmers and workmen, who soon would pass from the earth.

Studer's efforts came at a propitious moment. New York State had decided to modernize its water system and build a giant new reservoir at Ashokan, New York, to supply New York City as well as upstate New York. This meant that scores of old-timers would be displaced, as their old farms and homes were bought out by the state. I vividly recall, as a senior camper in the 1940s, riding in Studer's old station wagon throughout the region, sitting on the front porches of elderly workers whose homes were marked for destruction and listening to their stories. Strangely, the dismay we felt about how progress was affecting them never applied to what we read about in the USSR; the same people who taught us the downside of progress at home waxed ecstatic about the great dams that Stalin was building with slave labor.

Studer managed to turn up a few true folk artists. Camp Woodland's pride and joy was a man who came to be called "the bard of the Catskills," a tall, striking, weathered man discovered in his eighties, named George Edwards. Years later, his songs would be published in a book edited by the Communist composer Norman Cazden, another man who served on the camp's music staff. Entitled *A Catskill Songster,* the book would preserve Edwards' legacy, as would a recording put out by the camp's later song counselor, Bob DeCormier, called *Catskill Mountain Folksongs.* The camp had honored the locals and listened to their woes; so they were not about to turn their back on the camp. In their eyes, no doubt, the charges of communism hurled at Woodland appeared to be nothing but irrelevant publicity ploys by grandstanding congressmen trying to gain exposure for their reelection campaigns.

The camp also worked to acquaint us with people who back then were neglected fighters for civil rights. For instance, Bob DeCormier, a brilliant singer and composer, as well as a man of great feeling and charisma, wrote a cantata about the life of Sojourner Truth. Campers learned that the nearby Catskill community of Hurley (site of yet another, smaller Commie camp, Camp Hurley) was her birthplace. In addition to DeCormier's musical tribute, the camp unsuccessfully campaigned to have the site marked by a memorial statue.

At day's end each Saturday, there was a long night of square dancing, with calls provided by the old-timers we had so studiously courted, accompanied by counselors such as John Cohen, later to be a member of an old-time music group, the New Lost City Ramblers. Other singers and pickers at Woodland included the black writer Julius Lester, remembered fondly by his friends as having started out a folkie; and Eric Weissberg, one of the first New York bluegrass players, who gained fame with his "Dueling Banjos" for the film *Deliverance,* and later was a member of a Sixties folk group, the Tarriers. Later, Joe Hickerson, then a student at Oberlin College and a fine singer, would be there; eventually he would become the folk music archivist at the Library of Congress. And of course, no summer was complete without the arrival of Pete Seeger, who at times stayed at the camp for long periods.

Loyal Woodland alumni treasured their long summers of solidarity at camp: the passionate romances, the fights, the hikes and expeditions, and the competitive sporting events with other camps. Into these regular camp activities, the Communist propagandizing was effortlessly integrated. Rather than "color wars," Woodland had a "Summer Youth Festival," its own version of the international Communist Festival of World Youth held each year in a Communist country. At the Soviet bloc event, the young people would begin and end the festivities singing "The World Youth Song" by the Soviet composer Dimitri Shostakovich; so of course we sang it at Woodland, using the lyrics printed in *The People's Song Book.* It was a bright, lyrical tune promising better tomorrows when all would live in peace and harmony under socialism.

> Everywhere the youth are singing
> Freedom's Song, Freedom's Song, Freedom's Song.
> We are the Youth,
> And the World Acclaims our Song of Truth.

At Woodland, the competitive teams were divided into different nations. Of course, everyone vied for the honor of being with either the USSR or the People's Republic of China (never called Red China in our camp). The losers who were given the USA team could only sulk over their bad luck. Two of our campers, both friends of mine, were American-born Chinese, Emil and Carl Chi. Their father was Chi Ch'ao-ting, a longtime secret Communist in China, who had infiltrated and gained a high post in the Kuomintang, only to surface as a top Communist after Mao's victory. He had married an American, however, and his wife and children remained in this country, which is how the kids wound up at Camp Woodland. Carl and Emil assured me that if and when the United Nations took China's seat away from Taiwan and gave it to the People's Republic, then their father would be appointed China's ambassador to the U.N. and they would once again all be able to live together. They, and all we campers, proudly sang the Chinese Communist anthems we learned, such as "Chee Lai" or the "Song of the Volunteers," with its wonderful ode to Mao's troops: "We will follow you forever, till China will be free." The song, whose title is given in *The People's Song Book* as "Arise," tells us that the Chinese Communists were fighting for "true democracy." I'm certain that many of the campers were surprised decades later to watch what happened at Tiananmen Square.

It was during the weeks of the Summer Youth Festival that the most overt indoctrination took place. Each night, the camp presented lectures and discussions with visitors from different countries, purportedly there to acquaint us with the life and culture of their native lands. The summer I turned fourteen, two young men from Greece were the featured speakers. Their presentation, however, was not about Greece. Rather, they offered a clarion call on behalf of the Greek Communists and a heroic narrative of the activities of party cadre in Greece during the ill-fated civil war. In their telling, the Greek partisans, led by the Communist Party, fought the good fight against American-backed fascists and nobly sought to build a free Greece aligned with the USSR.

The presence of these guests also afforded the opportunity for camp staff to sound out who was truly sympathetic, and use the moment to try recruiting new members for the international

Communist movement. Their recruiting drive took place during rest period. Our counselor, an austere and authoritarian man named Bob Glass, gave us some good news: a chosen few of us would get to skip the daily, mandatory rest period if we came to a special presentation by our Greek guests. I recall that we left the bunk feeling very, very special. The two young men informed us that although we did not have the honor of fighting with arms for Communism as their compatriots did, we could be part of the same struggle in our own country. All we had to do was join the ranks of the Labor Youth League, as the youth group of the Communist Party USA was then called. Here, in the imperialist heartland, we young proletarians could be part of the international fight alongside seasoned Marxist-Leninists of other lands. Like these Greek heroes, we too could thus be part of the vanguard forces fighting to emancipate the workers of the world!

Lying on the grass at the bottom of a mountain slope in the Catskills, we dreamt of a revolutionary struggle that would be worthy of our new friends, the two Greek comrades. They took my name and address home with them. I never thought I would hear from them, and after returning to the city, quickly forgot the episode. Much to my dismay—and to the shock of my wary parents, who wanted to protect me from the possible backlash of what they thought was incipient fascism—one day the two arrived at my door without previous announcement and asked me to join them at a local meeting of the Labor Youth League, where I could formally join. I turned down the offer; there was something about their austere nature and fanatical commitment that scared me. But the seeds had been sown. A year or two later I sought out the youth arm of the party on my own, and became an active member of the Upper West Side chapter of the league.

On Sunday mornings, campers gathered at the amphitheater for our regular ecumenical convocation, a substitute for the religious services held at non-Commie camps. When the Korean War came to an end, we looked forward with anticipation to what we expected would be a tribute to those who had sought to end the war. We were not disappointed. Norman Studer spoke of how those of us who favored peace could be pleased with our work, and then we sang our favorite peace songs: "Study War No More" and "Strangest Dream," as well as "Put My Name Down," a song calling upon Americans to endorse the so-called Stockholm Peace Petition, a Soviet bloc initiative that demanded unilateral nuclear disarmament by the Western "imperialist" powers. The more militant among us envied what we imagined to be the response at a camp like Wo-Chi-Ca, where campers could openly say they sought victory for North Korea, a unified Communist nation, and defeat of the United States.

Among my fellow campers were many children of blacklisted entertainment industry figures, as well as the two sons of Ethel and Julius Rosenberg, who had been executed for "conspiracy to commit espionage." (In a strange twist of fate—given my own involvement later in the Rosenberg case—my parents gave the Rosenberg children's adoptive parents, Abel and Anne Meeropol, my old footlocker to use for the boys' clothes when they first went off to the camp.) We also had many of the children of Communist leaders incarcerated under the Smith Act, and some whose parents joined the ranks of the CP "underground" when its leaders sent their cadre into hiding in 1949, preparing for the war and the fascist repression they expected. My own bunkmate, Charlie Ehrenpreis, told me how he had to follow a complicated, prearranged plan for secret meetings with his stepfather, waiting at selected New York subway stops and watching for the arrival of a designated train, so they could speak briefly on the platform.

All of this brings to mind the line spoken by a character in Woody Allen's classic film *Annie Hall.* Like so many of her friends, she said, she attended "socialist summer camp." When queried about what that meant on a television game show, Allen's coauthor Marshall Brickman, my old college roommate, responded that it was a camp in which the kids competed by giving the most brownie points to those whose fathers had actually served time under the Smith Act, the law under which American Communist leaders were convicted for conspiring to "teach and advocate overthrow of the U.S. Government by force and violence."

3

The Little Red Schoolhouse

HAVING GRADUATED FROM ELEMENTARY SCHOOL IN WASHINGTON Heights, I was expected to move on to the local junior high—a school with a bad reputation, in a tough neighborhood, where Jewish students were an oppressed minority. Partly because they worried about what they regarded as my delicate emotional state and partly for political reasons, my parents inquired if there was an opening at Elisabeth Irwin, the high school affiliated with the Greenwich Village elementary school known as the Little Red Schoolhouse.

In New York City, of course, there existed then as now a wide choice of prestigious private schools, from the elite gem Horace Mann, to the Ethical Culture Society's famous Fieldston School, to other progressive education centers such as the Dalton School and Walden. But the factor that made EI (as everyone called Elisabeth Irwin) distinctive was that it was a refuge for teachers who would be thrown out of the public school system because they would not sign the Feinberg Law oath, stating that they were not members of the Communist Party; or because they had refused to testify when called before HUAC's investigation of the New York school system. There were fellow travelers as well as actual Communist Party members, along with a few independents from the non-Communist, but never the anti-Communist, New York Left. There was a reason why we called the institution we attended "the Little Red Schoolhouse for little Reds."

In the new alumni guide, the list of former students in both the elementary and the high school reads like a Who's Who of the Children of the Old Left. Among the graduates are Victor Navasky, now editorial director and publisher of *The Nation;*

Angela Davis, the African-American former Communist Party leader; Kathy Boudin, a leader of the Weather Underground now in prison for life for her part in the Brinks Weather Underground murders; author, singer and left-wing playwright Fred Gardner; book editor Daniel Menaker, also the author of a novel called *The Old Left;* the wives of both Harry Belafonte and Pete Seeger; Michael and Robert Meeropol, the sons of Ethel and Julius Rosenberg; my old college roommate and banjo player extraordinaire Eric Weissberg, whose hit song "Dueling Banjos" put bluegrass music on the map; the Broadway choreographer Julie Arenal Primus, whose relatives were involved in one of the plots to assassinate Leon Trotsky; and Joady and Nora Guthrie, two of Woody's children. Sometimes it seems that the question is, was there anyone of note who was part of the Old Left or the New Left who did *not* attend Elisabeth Irwin?

I entered EI in 1949 and graduated in 1955. Perhaps the highlight of my years there came at graduation time. We picked as our graduation speaker W. E. B. Du Bois, America's most famous Negro intellectual, a man whose career and life represented the trajectory of the movement for civil rights in black America. Du Bois was a founding member of the NAACP in the 1900s, editor of its journal *The Crisis* for many years, and the leading opponent of the conservative black nationalism advocated by Booker T. Washington. But we did not choose Du Bois because we valued these accomplishments; rather, we picked him because we knew him as a trusted leader of the pro-Communist Left, a friend of the Soviet Union, and therefore an advocate for "progressive" America. True, we had read his most famous work, *The Souls of Black Folk,* in our tenth-grade English class. But we also knew that Du Bois had been indicted by the United States government and put on trial for failing to register as a foreign agent, which his defenders argued was a ruse to put his Peace Information Center out of business, because the ruling class could not afford a real debate about the nature of American imperialism. In a legal and technical sense, he was not an agent of the USSR, but rather an "agent of influence" who sought through the media to gather support for the Soviet motherland.

Ironically, our class's choice of Du Bois as our graduation speaker created a mini-crisis for the school. Our principal was Randolph B. Smith, a native New Englander with the regal bearing of a Boston Brahmin. Clearly not a traditional Communist or even a fellow traveler, Smith was more a soft liberal who had been called to appear before the House Committee on Un-American Activities less because of his outspoken libertarianism than because of EI's reputation. The school's leadership worried that the choice of Du Bois as the official commencement speaker—this was the class of 1955, after all—could put EI under. Moreover, some prominent liberals like Max Lerner, an anti-Communist who wrote a regular column for the *New York Post* and who had a daughter at Elisabeth Irwin, were disturbed by the idea of Du Bois's appearance. Some of these parents threatened to boycott the ceremony.

I still remember the somber mood when Rank Smith (as our principal liked to be called) told us to choose another speaker. He explained that a commencement ceremony had to feature a speaker acceptable to everyone in the class, and that the majority who voted for Du Bois simply could not force their choice on the entire graduating class and its parent body. He offered us a compromise that we had no option but to accept: Du Bois would appear later at a compulsory, all-school assembly when the entire student body and interested parents could hear his message. That meeting eventually took place. I do not recall what it is Du Bois spoke about, but I'm sure he condemned the United States as a failed country that had abandoned democracy—his standard line during these years—and offered praise and salutations to the Communist countries, which were building the future of world socialism.

Our fallback choice for commencement speaker was Arthur Miller, whose play *The Crucible,* about witch hunts in colonial Salem, was a parable on McCarthyism. Miller's left-wing credentials were impeccable. In his speech he told us never to accept "half a loaf." We took that to mean that we should have demanded that Du Bois speak, and that the school's authorities were wrong to capitulate to pressure from objecting parents.

But a short time later, we learned what Miller must really have been thinking about. As the whole world was soon to know, he left his wife, a simple social worker, for America's leading Hollywood beauty queen, the incomparable Marilyn Monroe—"the whole loaf" incarnate.

Elisabeth Irwin's official seventy-fifth anniversary book, published in 1997, is a time capsule of the way we were. It is filled with alumni's memories, like this one by an unnamed graduate from the 1940s: "In January of 1945, we voted to finish history with Russian History instead of the last two years of American History. We were all pretty much left-leaning 'progressives' and thought Russia was great and Communism a noble experiment. Many flirted with Communism as an alternative." Another entry reads: "We served coffee to the Phelps Dodge strikers and worked hard for Henry Wallace in the 1948 Presidential election." One former student remembers that the McCarthy period was "a child's nightmare. Pete Seeger was blacklisted. One father who refused to testify before the McCarran Commission [the writer means Sen. Pat McCarran's Internal Security Subcommittee of the U.S. Senate] was fired from his U.N. job. Another was blacklisted in 1947.... Some of our teachers were victims of McCarthyism and could teach nowhere but at Little Red and Elisabeth Irwin. Many of us could have attended other schools.... We were the embattled ones, fighting for righteousness and the First Amendment."

In fact, as I have said, most of our teachers were proud Communists or fellow travelers rather than "victims." And the anonymous student was wrong about one other thing. The only "embattled" students at EI were mavericks like members of the Trotskyist Socialist Workers Party or followers of the neo-Freudian Marxist Wilhelm Reich. One of the former was a student named Bob Burke, whose aggressive Trotskyism led him to be shunned by his fellow students. Yet Burke was relentless, peddling *The Militant* and SWP literature, and refusing to shut up. Then one day he disappeared. Months later, there he was in front of a concert I attended, selling his party's newspaper. I asked what had happened to him; he replied that he had dropped out and moved to another school, since his anti-

Stalinism made him a pariah with both students and a hostile faculty at EI.

Over the years, I had two other encounters with Bob Burke. Once I spotted him in the audience at the famous debate in the late 1960s between Tom Hayden and Michael Harrington, on which more later. And then, in the late 1970s, I was speaking on a panel with Irving Howe about the fate of American socialism, and suddenly, Burke stood up and spoke during the question period. He was dressed in black cleric's garb, reversed collar and all. Was this a put-on? I had known Burke to be Jewish when he attended EI. I found him afterward and asked what was up. He explained that he had converted, attended theological school and received a degree, and he was now an ordained minister. But, he assured me, speaking slowly so I didn't miss the point, "In religion I'm a Christian, but in politics I'm still a Bolshevik!" Chalk another one up for old EI!

I have already mentioned the role that the Rosenberg case played in my life. At EI, my friends and I threw ourselves completely into the campaign for clemency. I became an active member of the Youth Committee for the Rosenbergs and their codefendant Morton Sobell, handing out leaflets in the streets of New York and traveling to the nation's capitol to picket the White House along with my friend and classmate Mary Travers. On the night of the Rosenbergs' execution, I stood amidst thousands of other New Yorkers who had gathered on East Seventeenth Street (the police had forbid the demonstrators to use Union Square) for a protest and vigil. To everyone connected to the school, it was simply a given truth that the Rosenbergs were innocent progressives who were murdered because of their dedication to peace.

Half a lifetime later, there is no indication in the school's anniversary book that most everyone now acknowledges that the Rosenbergs were in fact Soviet agents. One student proclaims:

> Hunting Communists was a major issue of the times. Most vivid are the emotion-filled discussions of the trial and execution of the Rosenbergs. We sat in circles with our classmates talking about it, and continued outside around the corner from Little

Red behind the newsstand. Only later did some of us learn that
the Rosenbergs' sons attended our school. [Actually, Michael and
Robert Meeropol attended the school after their parents were
executed, and after they had been legally adopted by Abel and
Anne Meeropol.] School was closed the day of the Julius and
Ethel Rosenberg execution as all the teachers were in Washington protesting. We were affected by the school's democratic
humanistic and altruistic spirit. It was an idealistic environment.

In fact, the Rosenbergs were executed on June 19, 1953, after EI
had closed for the summer. There was a small gathering in the
capitol, but most protesters were at the Seventeenth Street rally.
Nostalgia for the good old days had made EI appear even more
involved than it was—to prove how it was on the right side of
history.

Indeed, Elisabeth Irwin was rather successful in creating people who thought this way and whose thoughts remain petrified
through a lifetime. A few independent souls managed to avoid
this fate, but my own dogmatic Marxism was to a large degree
a result of my EI education. I remember in particular an austere,
authoritarian and extremely opinionated man who was both the
eleventh-grade homeroom teacher and the school's social studies and history teacher, and who heavily influenced me. I remember him proudly telling us that "Marx pointed out that history is
the queen of the social sciences." He taught everything, including the earth science course (taken by nonscientific students
instead of physics), from the perspective of dialectical materi-
alism, which he presented as the unifying philosophical frame-
work explaining everything. The entry in the official anniversary
book states that this man "could make a complex era intelligi-
ble, without oversimplifying. He involved us by injecting strong
opinions and controversy in every class. He was a compact, very
intense and very stern man who loved history and gave us a wide
perspective that most don't get until college."

In addition to classroom indoctrination, we also had field
trips that today would be called politically correct. On one trip,
either the eleventh- or twelfth-grade excursion, we traveled to
the coal fields and steel towns of old blue-collar Pennsylvania,
now on the verge of extinction. One of the entries in the anniversary book recalls:

Anthracite and bituminous coal mines, slag heaps, steel mills. The containers of molten steel overhead were frightening. The nighttime view of open-hearth steel mills in Pittsburgh was unforgettable. At the Bethlehem Steel mill the whole class climbed into the gargantuan steam shovel used for strip mining. [I guess we didn't realize then that strip mining was anti-environmental.] One classmate exclaimed, "this must be God." Meeting coal miners' union head, John L. Lewis, was an unforgettable moment. So was riding in the elevator down the long coalmine shaft into the total black, the daylight disappearing above us. In the pitch dark at the bottom we sang "Dark as a Dungeon" to keep from being afraid.

My recollection of the trip differs slightly from this. Indeed, we did sing "Dark as a Dungeon," the classic ode to coal mining written by the master guitar picker, the late Merle Travis. Led by our charismatic music teacher, Bob DeCormier, we sang this ballad and other left-wing songs for the miners, whom I remember as being both bemused and totally oblivious to our political message. The incongruity of a bunch of middle-class New York City high school kids singing "Which Side Are You On?"—the best-known of the Communist anthems of the 1930s—to actual coal miners who probably envied our chances in life, and yet were thankful that they had a job and a decent wage, simply did not occur to us.

On the same trip, there was another brief but embarrassing moment. We were taken to a local working-class Catholic church, where we met a priest who tended to the spiritual needs of his local congregation. The problem was that he insisted on telling us about the Miracle of the Lady of Fatima, who appeared to local Polish peasants to warn them about the coming threat of communism. I can still remember the snickers emanating from our ranks and the chagrin of our teachers who, having extolled the merits of working-class consciousness, now had to remain silent.

To be fair, it is important to acknowledge that there were good and dedicated teachers at EI. Our English teacher, Ed Stillman, a proud member of the non-Communist Left, taught us to love and respect good literature. A tough and demanding taskmaster, he assigned the great classics and made us appreciate them. One of my good friends, Hank Lifson, wrote in the anniversary book that Stillman "made the writings of Thoreau, Emerson, Hawthorne and Melville alive for us as we visited the sites where they lived and the places they wrote about." I fully concur. On our twelfth-grade trip to New England, we read Thoreau on the shores of Walden Pond, and we visited the whaling villages that Melville wrote about in *Moby Dick*. Literature came to life with Ed Stillman. Moreover, although he was a charter member of the anti-anti-Communist Emergency Civil Liberties Committee, a group chaired by the fellow traveler Corliss Lamont, Stillman was definitely not a Leninist. When I wrote a crude tract opposing "bourgeois" civil liberties, Stillman criticized my work mercilessly and had me read John Locke and Milton in order to learn the necessity of intellectual freedom.

Of all the teachers at EI, the ninth-grade homeroom teacher, Bob Leicester, was the most important to me personally. Bob was a warm, cheerful and forceful personality. He was informal, friendly and caring, and he dedicated himself to teaching us how the political system worked. Under Bob's tutelage, we actually took roles in the New York mayoralty race, and held a schoolwide debate in which class members represented the positions of the major candidates. That was the year a politician named Rudolph Halley, now all but forgotten, made a name for himself as a tough reformer, fighting both organized crime and the political machines. I interviewed him for the school paper and chose to stand in for his platform in the school debate.

Bob Leicester was probably also a Communist, and once he asked me to inquire if my parents would make a contribution for the defense of the arrested Communist Party leaders. He also at one point ran for office himself on the ticket of the pro-Communist American Labor Party. Then, finally, Bob almost got in trouble. He was a contestant on *The $64,000 Question,* the famous quiz show of the 1950s. (He won on what for him was a dead giveaway question: "Who was Heywood Broun?" A famous left-wing journalist, Broun was probably Bob's friend.) A local gossip columnist ran an item revealing Bob's political record and asked how a respected quiz show could not only let someone like him on the air but also let him win. As the congressional quiz-

show hearings that would cost Mark Van Doren his job and reputation began, EI suddenly decided to give Bob a sabbatical
leave, although school was in session. Bob left for a European
vacation with his family, and returned only after the hearings had
concluded.

In addition to learning the party line at the Little Red Schoolhouse, I spent a good deal of time hanging around the Village
and going to Washington Square on Sundays for the weekly folk
music gatherings, and to parties at people's homes where we
heard some of the first generation of city-bred country pickers
and folk singers whose names would later become household
words. Foremost among them, the man who inspired virtually
everyone, was Pete Seeger, whom I had already gotten to know
at Woodland. We all had what at that point was Pete's only
album, his 1948 LP on Folkways Records, which made him a folk
legend. With his high tenor voice, crackling banjo played frail-
ing style and head thrown back with his Adam's apple bobbing
as he sang, Pete was our Elvis Presley.

Seeger was also big at Elisabeth Irwin High School, where it
was assumed that folk music was the "authentic voice of the people." The school's music program was led by Bob DeCormier,
a charming, handsome and talented singer and choral director
who went on to lead the New York Choral Society and then
(under the *nom de plume* Robert Corman) the Harry Belafonte
Singers during Belafonte's heyday; and he was the music
arranger for Peter, Paul and Mary. While he was at EI,
DeCormier also directed a chorus I had joined, the Jewish Young
Folk-Singers (the JYF), which was affiliated with the International
Workers Order, a fraternal order created by the Communist
Party.

The most cherished JYF performance was of Shostakovich's
Stalinist anthem "Song of the Forests." We also excelled at performing folk cantatas, such as Earl Robinson's "Lonesome Train"
and his most famous composition, "Ballad for Americans." We
performed the latter many times, once with Paul Robeson recre-
ating his wartime performance for a benefit concert for the
Labor Youth League during its annual convention. Robeson had

even sung the cantata at the 1944 Republican National Convention. In those days, the composition reflected the theme of wartime unity of American democracy against the threat of fascism—we're all Americans, it said, united regardless of race and religion. In the 1950s, it symbolized something very different: the standing fast of American Communists behind their creed, and the myth that only the party represented the best of the American tradition, which McCarthyite fascism was destroying. Indeed, at the end of the chorale, an actor appeared onstage to read aloud Langston Hughes' most sectarian Communist poem, "Let America Be America Again"—the only time Hughes argued on behalf of a soviet America.

I resolved to become a real folk singer and banjo player. Fortunately, Pete Seeger was giving group banjo lessons in the East Village, across the street from the Downtown Community School, where he taught music twice a week. For one year, Pete taught a small group of five or so students, at the princely sum of two dollars for a four- or five-hour class. Eric Weissberg, already a whiz, attended very briefly, but since he already knew as much banjo as Seeger, he quickly left the group. Another student was Vladimir Posner, who later became Gorbachev's voice in America during the last dying gasp of Communism.

Seeger was my hero. Often he would stay in my parents' New York City apartment when he was in town, since it was a long commute to home in Beacon, New York. Pete and I would head to my apartment after the lesson, and he would make music on the subway ride home. On a bus once, he remarked how musical the window wipers sounded as they swept away the rain. Like other left-wing youth, I made the pilgrimage to Pete's home, which he said he had built in the 1940s with the help of other young people in the folk and Communist movements. He lived high up on a mountain, and had to meet us at the bottom to drive us up in his jeep. We spent the day there, singing, eating and having a good time. Among the guests was the Communist hack writer Michael Gold, née Granich, who wrote one noteworthy book in his entire career, *Jews Without Money*, now important only as a relic of proletarian literature that reflected an

immigrant milieu. Gold had become one of the CP's top pro-
pagandists, and wrote a weekly column for the *Daily Worker*
called "Change the World." After that picnic at Pete's, Gold was
struck by how many of us New York teens worshipped Seeger,
whom he dubbed "the Karl Marx of the teenagers."

It was not a comparison that Pete rejected; indeed, he was
probably flattered by it. At one of my banjo lessons I noticed that
Pete's banjo case was stuffed with a week's worth of the *Daily
Worker.* "They're to take to the hospital and read aloud to
Woody," he proudly told me. His hero and mentor Woody
Guthrie, then suffering the horrible results of Huntington's
chorea and largely confined to Brooklyn State Hospital, had to
be kept in touch with the party line.

Today, Pete is a national institution. As he arrived in town to
receive his Kennedy Center Honors award in 1995, as well as a
Medal of Honor in the Arts from President Bill Clinton, a puff
piece in the *Washington Post* proclaimed him "America's best-
loved Commie." Pete is widely regarded as an eccentric, somewhat harmless idealist, filled with good intentions. At the
Kennedy Center gala, a brief film about Seeger told viewers how
during the Great Depression he sang protest songs, as the sound-
track played the Almanac Singers' version of "Which Side Are
You On?" The ceremony also praised Pete's refusal to capitulate
to the witch hunters, alluding to his decision to invoke the First
Amendment, rather than the Fifth, when he declined to testify
before HUAC in the 1960s. And we were informed of his "pro-
union and antifascist songs."

But somehow, the award makers forgot to tell everyone about
Seeger's most famous record—the Almanac Singers' very first
album—*Songs for John Doe*. Released during the week in June
1941 when Hitler broke his pact with Stalin and invaded the
USSR, the antiwar album was filled with hard-hitting songs that
called for no intervention in European battles on behalf of
British imperialism, and condemned Roosevelt as a warmon-
gering fascist who worked for J. P. Morgan. "I hate war, and so
does Eleanor, and we won't be safe till everybody's dead," went
a rollicking verse to the tune of "Jesse James." Another, written

to the melody of an old country tune, "Cripple Creek," proclaimed "Franklin D., Franklin D., you ain't gonna send us 'cross the sea." It was pure party-line propaganda.

A writer for the *Atlantic Monthly* appropriately panned the album when it was released, calling it an offense to "the American defense effort, democracy and the army." The reason so few people know of the album's existence is easily explained: In true Communist fashion, Pete and his comrades had to respond immediately to the change in the party line that occurred when Hitler invaded the USSR. That meant a recall of the album just beginning to be produced. All pressings were destroyed, leaving only a few for posterity. Soon the Almanacs released an apology, "Dear Mr. President," in which Pete lamented, in the understatement of the time, "Dear Mr. President, we haven't always agreed in the past, I know," and went on to say he was ready to "turn in my banjo for something that makes a little more noise," i.e., a machine gun.

My friend Pete, then, was not just another antiwar activist. He was for peace during the Nazi-Soviet Pact, but called for U.S. intervention in the war after the Soviet Union was invaded. Then during the Cold War, when Stalin tried to expand the Soviet sphere in Europe, the time had come to order a new peace offensive. So Seeger made the transition from war to peace songs, bolstering the Soviet Union's Stockholm Peace Petition, which called for unilateral Western disarmament. "Put my name down, brother, where do I sign, I'm going to join the fight for peace, right down the line."

Of course, Seeger had his own problems with the party, which never really trusted its own most favored artists—with the exception, perhaps, of the formidable Paul Robeson. For one thing, Seeger had the temerity to form a commercial group named the Weavers, which got on the Hit Parade in the late 1940s with "Goodnight, Irene," the hora "Tzena, Tzena," the traditional "On Top of Old Smokey," and Leadbelly's classic, rewritten with new words, "Kisses Sweeter Than Wine." The onset of the blacklist cooled the group's career, which only picked up in the late 1950s, as the Weavers gained a new audience of leftists in the folk revival that functioned as a prelude to the Sixties.

Ironically, just as the blacklist was being developed, the Weavers got caught up in an internal CP issue: the party's campaign against "white chauvinism," when scores of white party members found themselves caught up in a war among the leadership, whose doomsday weapon was the accusation of racism. Party apparatchik Irwin Silber became the editor of *Sing Out!*, a folk music magazine which soon deteriorated into a sectarian publication for musical propaganda. On the side of the party leaders in the internecine conflict, Silber blasted the Weavers as racists for singing the songs of Negro America without having a black member. I remember asking Pete about this after a lesson. "Irwin is a literary type, not a folkie," he responded, as if that answered the question. (Years later, Silber would be the first to condemn Bob Dylan for "betraying" the folk movement by going electric. Some believe that Dylan's "Mr. Jones" was written about Silber—"There's something happening here and you don't know what it is, Do You, Mr. Jones?") Shortly thereafter, Silber created a Weavers copycat group called the Gateway Singers, whose female singer was black. When the quartet performed at Carnegie Hall, the audience practically laughed them out of the auditorium.

Pete was caught up in all this infighting but he never seemed to become disillusioned. And he never criticized the Soviet Union. A few years ago, he told his biographer David King Dunaway that he now realized Stalin was a "hard driver"—quite a mild rebuke for perhaps the bloodiest of the twentieth-century dictators. As Dunaway wrote in his very sympathetic portrait of Seeger, "Decades after quitting the Party, [Seeger's] harshest criticism of the Stalin era was an 'awful lot of rough stuff.'" Recently, a PBS special about him found Seeger telling Bill Moyers that we must never forget the crimes of the past. He then sang an uninspired new song about the Nazi camp at Treblinka. One might pause to ask—Moyers, of course, did not—whether Seeger would ever consider composing a similar song about the Soviet Gulag.

Indeed, throughout the 1950s and '60s, long after Stalin's war against the Jews had become well known, Pete would sing "Hey Zhankoye," for which he wrote his own English lyrics. Originally a Soviet ballad in Yiddish, it recounted the fiction that Stalin had

freed the Jews of Russia and had settled them in a new Jewish
socialist colony in Birobidzhan, Stalin's answer to "reactionary
Zionism." Pete's verses tell us:

> When you go from Sevastopol,
> On the way to Simforopol,
> Just you go a little further down,
> There's a little railroad depot
> Known quite well by all the people,
> Called Zhankoye, Zhan, Zhan, Zhan.

> Now if you look for paradise,
> You'll see it there before your eyes;
> Stop your search and go no further on.
> There we have a collective farm
> All run by husky Jewish arms
> At Zhankoye, Zhan, Zhan, Zhan.

In reality Birobidzhan was a completely failed experiment in
which Jews were given virtually useless land, barely yielding a
livelihood. Seeger used to sing "Hey Zhankoye" long after the
Yiddish poet Peretz Markish was arrested as "an enemy of the
people, American spy and Zionist agent." I've always wondered
if Seeger ever read Arkady Vaksberg's powerful book *Stalin
Against the Jews,* which describes Stalin's murder of the Yiddish
poets he once revered, Solomon Mikhoels and Itzik Feffer.

Pete's argument has always been that although he may have
been wrong, he only acted out of love for his country. That is
why, he has often said, he opposed the war in Vietnam. But in
fact, as Voltaire said of God, Vietnam is something Pete Seeger
would have had to invent if it hadn't existed. For it was Vietnam
that brought Pete back into the mainstream. The broad and
effective antiwar movement was waiting to welcome him and the
other 1950s Communists back home. And Pete wrote a song that
became the movement's Vietnam anthem, "Waist Deep in the
Big Muddy," with its harsh judgment on LBJ—"and the big fool
said to push on." In the mid-Sixties, Pete was booked to sing it
on *The Smothers Brothers* program on television, but the CBS censors cut out his performance. It took a year of protest for him to
be invited back and finally get to sing it on the airwaves. Still,

one could be against the war—many were—and not write the
kind of lyric Pete sang about Ho Chi Minh:

> He educated all the people,
> He demonstrated to the world,
> If a man will stand for his own land,
> He's got the strength of ten.

But all this was in the future. As a teenager, I loved Pete and
I loved music. He introduced me to the five-string banjo, and
folk music became a large part of my teen and college life. Each
Sunday my friends and I gathered at Washington Square Park,
where with police department permit in hand, we sang and
picked from noon to 5 P.M. in the spring and summer months.
There I came in contact with the luminaries of the early folk
scene, including Erik Darling, Ramblin' Jack Elliott (born Elliott
Charles Adnopoz), Happy and Artie Traum, Roy Berkeley and
others. One Sunday in 1954, Elliott came to the square with
none other than the legendary Woody Guthrie, and announced
that they were going to hitchhike across the country. Woody
attempted to sing some of his songs, but because he was already
suffering the effects of his terminal disease, he finally gave up,
and Elliott took over. I did get a chance to engage Woody in conversation about folk and the folk scene, and remember that he
told me how disillusioned he was about the quality of the music
being produced by the sectarian Communist movement of the
1950s. With unkempt clothing and a scraggly beard, Woody
looked nothing like his early photos. A policeman, thinking he
was drunk and a dangerous derelict, attempted to arrest him.
A crowd quickly gathered in protest, and Ramblin' Jack
informed the cop that Woody was a living legend, a man who
had been featured in the pages of *Life* magazine. The cop
quickly relented, saving Woody the embarrassment of a public
arrest.

With me at Washington Square that day were my friends Carl
Granich, the son of Mike Gold; Bob Starobin, the son of Joe
Starobin, the *Daily Worker*'s foreign editor and one of the first to
quit the American Communist Party in the late 1950s; and Mary

Travers, my classmate who would later be part of the famed Peter, Paul and Mary trio. Mary came from a radical family. Her father was the little-remembered "proletarian" novelist Robert Travers, and she had a strong voice as well as extremely good looks.

Mary was an outgoing and vivacious young girl. Her precocious sexuality continually got her in trouble, especially at school. One spring weekend, my friend Bob Orlins, Mary and I went to a classical music concert at the now destroyed Lewisohn Stadium, the fabled outdoor arena where New Yorkers could hear the best symphony orchestras (with regular interruptions by passing airplanes). It was a beautiful evening, brought to a quick end by a sudden downpour that soaked us to the skin. I told my parents that I was going to Bob's house in Brooklyn; we descended instead to Mary's home in the Village, where Bob quickly disappeared with Mary while I found myself being vamped by her thirteen-year-old stepsister. Mary also caused a scandal by appearing scantily clad in the pages of a pre-*Playboy* sex photo tabloid, which she brought to class and proudly displayed to all who wanted a look.

Today, Mary is regularly heralded as one of Elisabeth Irwin's top graduates. She has endowed a music scholarship in the name of the elementary school teacher who introduced her to folk music, and she performs and raises funds for the school. But she actually did not graduate from Elisabeth Irwin. In the eleventh grade, Mary was expelled. Each day, until her transfer to a public high school was arranged, she stood on the street in front of the school building—her own brownstone was directly opposite the main entrance—and yelled taunts to our class, which faced the street. Our teachers implored us to ignore her, and tried to draw an object lesson about people whose behavior was bad enough to be removed from the premises. But in the officially rewritten history of the school, Mary Travers now is regularly portrayed as one of the institution's most distinguished graduates, the truth about her school years conveniently forgotten.

It was only a matter of time before I would join the Communist Party's youth movement, then called the Labor Youth League.

Why did I finally sign up, after hesitantly refusing the overtures of the two Greek revolutionaries who had tried to recruit me at Camp Woodland? Looking back, I think the reasons had little to do with politics, and a great deal to do with the need to find an identity. Strangely, belonging to the LYL served that purpose. It provided the camaraderie of a tight-knit group of ready-made friends, along with a sense of moral superiority, of being on the right side of a good fight most people didn't even know about. And it offered the possibility of what every teenage boy seeks: a girlfriend. God bless the Communist movement for giving me my very first sexual experiences from among a group of "liberated" girls whom I found time to romance when not engaging in fundraising for the *Daily Worker* or riding in American Labor Party sound trucks during election week.

Most of the members of my branch, the Upper West Side LYL, were all Jewish. Another shared aspect of that Jewish upbringing was a purely cultural *Yiddishkeit* that emphasized Yiddish literature and theater, the folk writing of Sholom Aleichem, the parables of freedom that abounded throughout Jewish culture, and most important, a complete rejection of anything to do with religion. Except for the rare occasion when I had to attend a relative's or friend's bar mitzvah, I never set foot in a synagogue, and learned nothing about Jewish doctrine, ritual or prayer. An old joke in Communist circles was: "What Jewish holidays do you celebrate?" "Paul Robeson's birthday and May Day."

Our West Side club convened once a week, rotating our meetings through different members' apartments. Our activities included going through housing projects in Harlem selling copies of the league's mass publication, *New Horizons,* to many residents who undoubtedly had better things to do with their hard-earned money. We campaigned for New York City's "third party," the so-called American Labor Party, which by the 1950s had become nothing but a poorly disguised Communist front; for a time, its sole member of the House of Representatives, the legendary Vito Marcantonio, spouted the "progressive" line in Washington, D.C. We also gathered used clothing to be sold in bazaars for the American-Soviet Friendship Council.

It was at a local LYL club meeting that I first met David Horowitz, who would become my lifelong friend. Traveling to the meeting from his home in Sunnyside, Queens, David told us that he had been appointed the official youth editor of the *Daily Worker,* and hence was making the rounds to recruit people to submit articles for publication. I was struck by David's poise, confidence and sophisticated knowledge of the intricacies of party policy and program. I recall that we all sat in awe before him, not knowing what to say or how to respond to his queries. I did, however, take seriously the offer to do some writing and began looking for something I could contribute.

The chance came when my high school was chosen to participate in a mock United Nations session, which was actually held in the General Assembly room of the United Nations on East Forty-second Street. "Delegates" from the different private and public schools in New York City were to debate the issues of the day as if we represented the positions of different nations. Of course, rather than truly represent the real positions taken by these nations, my comrades and I saw the chance to score a propaganda coup—by voting to take a position favored by the Soviet bloc, which it hadn't a ghost of a chance of passing in an actual U.N. session. My friend Hank Lifson and I introduced a resolution demanding admission to the U.N. for the People's Republic of China, which in those days was usually referred to as Red China. I do not recall what country we were supposedly representing, but the story I wrote for David Horowitz appeared in the *Daily Worker* without a byline, to protect me. It was my first published article.

The activities of the league were meant to prepare one for eventual admission to the CPUSA. Thus, each meeting began with "criticism and self-criticism" sessions, evidently modeled after those developed by Mao in China. One of our members was a young Chinese girl named Prudy Hoy, who told us that she would eventually return to China now that the Communists were in power. She led our group, and I recall being terrified when it came my turn to speak. Other members spoke about various inappropriate behavior they had engaged in, such as not working hard enough in school, where a good future Communist ought to excel; we could not merely act like ordinary bourgeois Americans. Not knowing what to say, I blurted out that all good young Communists should regularly read and engage in theoretical debates, as found in the party's journal, *Political Affairs*. Because I was undoubtedly the only member who even read this stuff, in addition to Sweezy and Huberman's unorthodox Marxist journal *Monthly Review*, my comments swept the group off its feet. I found myself quickly elected chairman of the local, because I alone could serve as guardian of the correct policy to be emulated by the youth.

Another good friend from the New York LYL was Bob Williamson, son of the CP's labor chief, the Scottish-born John Williamson. Indicted under the Smith Act, the senior Williamson had chosen to accept deportation to Britain instead of a trial and certain imprisonment. The British government provided him and his family first-class passage to London on the Queen Elizabeth, so I went with a few other close friends from the league to see him off. The next day's *Daily News* had a front-page picture of the Williamsons waving to us from the ship's deck, under the heading "Red Sails in the Sunset."

Bob was a taciturn, ultraserious revolutionary, constantly engaging in talk about the party and its leading role. I first met Bob as a bunkmate and co-counselor at Camp Bronx House–Emanuel, a summer camp run by the Federation of Jewish Philanthropies and affiliated with a well-known settlement house. Bronx House was not, like Woodland, a Red-diaper-baby camp; rather, it served the needs of working-class and poor Jews, as well as black and Puerto Rican youngsters, who got to attend the camp practically free of charge.

Williamson and I had a third roommate named Bob Shuchman. Ironically, Shuchman was not a Red-diaper baby, but a premature conservative and libertarian. He sometimes sadly admitted that his parents were New Deal Democrats. Before his premature death from a stroke in his twenties, he founded the Young Americans for Freedom (YAF), a group whose initial conference in Sharon, Connecticut, was hosted by their inspiration, the young William F. Buckley Jr.

Shuchman had the same day off as I did, so we would spend it together. Once, we hitched a ride from the camp to Tanglewood, a brief few hours away, and went to a hotel called the Music Inn, where Mahalia Jackson was singing along with the blues harmonica player Sonny Terry. We found out that a transvestite singer was doing a warmup, and that the hotel was a major gay hangout—in an era when, to our puritanical eyes, this was something not to be countenanced. Returning to camp proved far more eventful, and frightening. Hitchhiking was illegal, and as we walked down the road we saw that a car was following us closely. Not realizing it was the state police, Shuchman and I ran onto the grounds of a high school, with the car following us onto the grass. We stopped dead in our tracks. The cops stepped out of the car and said we had to walk back to camp. This took us six long hours, as the police car trailed behind us to make sure we didn't try to hitch another ride. All the while, as Shuchman and I condemned the fascist tactics of the police, he gave me an introduction to libertarianism. Bob argued that in a just society, anyone should be able to do anything that did no harm to others, and that the state had no right to interfere. I countered that the state had a right to impose a just order, and that what we were experiencing was simply a case of the abuse of power.

It turned out that Bob Williamson talked in his sleep, and he made me promise to awaken him lest he inadvertently spill party secrets while Shuchman, the anti-Communist, could be taking it all in. Shuchman rose to the occasion and started to taunt Williamson every morning with the tidbits heard the night before. Each morning a fight broke out when Shuchman threatened to report his findings to a man he claimed he knew well, Herbert Philbrick, an FBI agent who had infiltrated the Communist Party and deceived his family into believing he was a Communist. Philbrick became famous through a television series based on his story, *I Led Three Lives*.

I also managed to take extracurricular classes at the Communist Party's educational institution, named—of course—the Jefferson School of Social Science. I always wondered how Thomas Jefferson would have felt had he been around to see that after Joseph Stalin's death, the windows of the school were festooned with life-size images of the Soviet dictator. I decided to take a course in American history from Herbert Aptheker, dean of the party historians, who had achieved some notoriety for his doctoral dissertation on American black slave revolts. During one of his classes, I happened to be eating candy, and unfortunately for me, it was a fudge bar in the shape of babies, named "Chocolate Babies." I had always assumed they were so named because they were images of babies, and were chocolate. But Aptheker exploded when he noticed the box at my desk. Summoning me to the front of the class, he used me as an example of how the evil of racism had infected even the most class-conscious young people in America. He took the box away and expelled me from class, saying that I could return only after I had examined my chauvinism and recanted, a process that had to take at least a few weeks. I often wondered whether, in the privacy of his own apartment, Aptheker surreptitiously ate the remainder of the confiscated box of "Chocolate Babies."

The most dramatic moment of my high school years was the execution of Julius and Ethel Rosenberg. We were bewildered that their trial was almost completely ignored by the Communist Party USA. Reading the *Daily Worker*, one might not even know that the event was producing banner headlines throughout the nation. The first impulse of the party's leadership, knowing of Julius's involvement in Soviet espionage, was to attempt to protect their movement by severing all association with the Rosenbergs. Yet despite this disloyalty, the Rosenbergs held fast. Had the couple admitted their guilt and become cooperative witnesses, the party would have been demolished overnight.

But once the fellow travelers at the *National Guardian* began their long campaign to prove the Rosenbergs' innocence, and it was clear that Julius and Ethel Rosenberg would cooperate in their portrayal as innocent martyrs and not say a word about their membership, the party leadership decided to put all their effort into creating a broad movement on the Rosenbergs' behalf. That decision coincided with Stalin's need to force attention away from the new anti-Semitic purge trials taking place in Czechoslovakia, where Rudolf Slansky and his comrades were sentenced to death. Indeed, the international Rosenberg defense committee was founded in Paris on December 3, 1952—the very day that Slansky and ten other former leading Czech Communists were executed in Prague. The explanation offered by Jacques Duclos, the staunchly pro-Stalinist head of the French Communist Party, was that "the conviction of U.S. atom spies Julius and Ethel Rosenberg was an example of anti-Semitism but the execution of eight Jews in Czechoslovakia last week was not."

In the United States, the esteemed party historian Herbert Aptheker quickly followed suit, writing that while the Slansky trial carried "no anti-Jewish aspect," anti-Semitism "played and plays a part" in the Rosenberg case. After all, he observed, in the Slansky trial the defendants "confess[ed] their guilt." Similarly, the Communist novelist Howard Fast, writing for a French audience, denounced the "stale smell of fascism" that the "Jewish masses of our country ... detected around Eisenhower," whose administration had made the Rosenbergs "hostages of the American peace movement."

I believed these charges. For me and the rest of the LYL members, the defense campaign on behalf of the Rosenbergs became the focus of our mass activity. All members of the league immediately joined the so-called Youth Committee to Secure Justice for the Rosenbergs and Sobell. Leading the group was codefendant Morton Sobell's stepdaughter, Sydney Gurewitz. Sydney lived through the trauma of her father's capture during their supposed "vacation" in Mexico, where Sobell had fled while trying to arrange for departure to Czechoslovakia.

Our work consisted of trying to convince New York's Jewish population—still only a few years away from the Nazi Holocaust—that America was now "fascist" and was trying to execute two Jews for their "progressive" political beliefs. And for second- and third-generation immigrant Jews like my friends and myself, the Rosenbergs' fate could just as well have been that of our own parents. My mother and father, after all, were also progressive activists steeped in the secular *Yiddishkayt* culture, people who cared for the Russians, who favored civil rights for Negroes, and who had fought in or supported the valiant fight of the Abraham Lincoln Brigade against fascism in Spain. We convinced ourselves that unless the decision to execute the Rosenbergs was overturned, the same fate might await our own loved ones.

And therefore I often found myself on New York City's streets, handing out leaflets that demanded a new trial and political amnesty for the condemned couple. We would seize each new "revelation" by William J. Reuben, the reporter who created the first conspiracy theory of the case (that the U.S. government had framed the Rosenbergs and forced the key government witness, Harry Gold, to lie on the witness stand), and then try to influence the average, nonprogressive Jews to participate in our fight. In support of the Rosenbergs, some of us once took a chartered train to Washington, D.C., an expedition captured in a now famous front-page photo in the *Daily News,* which shows us passing by coffins unloaded at the station—the coffins of American GIs being returned from Korea. We were convinced that the juxtaposition was not accidental, and that the forces running the government had purposefully scheduled these events in order to depict us as traitors responsible for the soldiers' deaths. For our part, we firmly believed that the GIs had died because of what Howard Fast called the "American imperialist aggression in Korea," and that the Rosenbergs were being killed because they had opposed our own government's crusade to crush socialism in the Far East. As Bob Cohen, one of my EI friends who took part in the Washington event, said to me, "We don't want peace in Korea; we want the North Koreans to win."

On the fatal evening of June 19, 1953, after all remaining legal avenues had been exhausted and before the sundown of the Jewish Sabbath, Ethel and Julius Rosenberg were to be electrocuted in New York's Sing Sing prison. It was time for the final vigil. Along with some ten or twelve thousand others, I headed to New York's Seventeenth Street, off Union Square, to gather in the naïve hope that our mere presence would prevent the execution. I recall feeling sure that our solidarity and our concern, shared the whole world over by the forces of peace and socialism, would put a stop to this brutal, inhumane execution, but a foretaste of the full fascism to come. We stood with tears in our eyes, ignoring the thundering words of the speakers and continuing to weep at the Negro ballads sung by Communist Party folk singers. Finally, Howard Fast appeared to tell us that the unspeakable was occurring: the Rosenbergs were being taken to the execution chamber. The photo of the event shows Fast at the sound truck's platform with William J. Patterson, head of the Civil Rights Congress, a CP front group, standing alongside. With Fast's announcement, tears turned into a wail of heavy crying and moaning, and the singers started chanting the old hymn of slavery in Egypt land, "Let My People Go."

The actual execution cut us adrift. Not knowing what to do, we marched with the crowd toward the Lower East Side, the last home of the Rosenbergs before they were sent to prison. Soon the police came on horseback, forcing us back and making us disperse. We saw the appearance of the mounted police as a reprise of the Russian Cossacks attacking the Jewish poor of the *shtetl*. The next morning, I met the members of my LYL club and journeyed to the funeral, where we stood with others outside the parlor, watching the hearse take the bodies to their final resting place. That moment would remain etched in my memory, forever to be the symbol of what awaited good, progressive Jews who dared to stand up for their beliefs. It would take almost forty years for me to face up to the real meaning of the Rosenberg case for America.

4

The Red Campus
in the Post-McCarthy Era

I ARRIVED IN MADISON, WISCONSIN, FOR COLLEGE IN SEPTEMBER 1955, along with my Elisabeth Irwin classmate Hank Lifson. We had decided to share a room in a small rooming house owned by the proprietor of the city's only record store. While most of my friends from the Labor Youth League had more or less automatically enrolled in the City College of New York, I had chosen the University of Wisconsin for two reasons: it had no math requirement, and it was the only campus in the country with an openly recognized chapter of the Labor Youth League.

Coming to a massive state university from a small private school in New York City was a culture shock. Fortunately I had Hank. Like me, he came from an ardently left-wing fellow-traveling family. But he studied painting diligently, had gone to the Art Student's League in New York, and was determined to make his life in the field of art. I, on the other hand, came to Madison with the desire to study history—the queen of the sciences, according to Marx—and to become a leader in the American Communist movement.

The LYL gave me a ready-made community, a group of friends, many of them already well established as student activists. I had been given a list of names by my friend Avi's brother, Henry Wortis, whose best friend, Arnie Lieber, had been a leader of the campus LYL before I arrived. As soon as I unpacked and checked out the campus, I began to call the people on his list. I first reached a young history graduate student, Marty Sklar, who would become a prominent American economic historian, and whose warm welcome calmed my newcomer anxieties. Marty was about to be married to a young black woman named Dori, and although I had just met him, he invited me to his wedding. Indeed, he not only invited me, but mentioned that he didn't have a suit to wear and asked if I by any chance had one. For some reason, I had brought my graduation suit to Madison, and it was about the right size, so I handed it over. This event was the first occasion in Madison when I met the other members of the Communist youth movement, most of whom were "secret" members who had not publicly acknowledged their commitment.

When Marty asked about my plans for college, I told him, "I want to be a leader in the Movement, and I'm ready and willing to assume an open position on campus as an LYL leader." His response was not what I expected to hear. "I think you should take a good deal of time and think this over carefully," he said. "That step could affect your entire life, and close off many opportunities in your future. You might not even be able to get a job. You can serve the Movement easily in other ways." His words sounded as though they were coming from my parents, and I was obstinate. "I made the decision about what to do with my life in high school," I responded, "and I fully intend to serve the working class. That's my only goal." Nothing Marty said could change my decision. He conferred with others in the LYL leadership—I was informed who they were—and shortly he told me that indeed, if I was certain about my decision, I could become the secretary-treasurer of the Labor Youth League. The chairman was Jerry Fiderer, a lanky and frenetic upperclassman who gave the appearance of someone on speed.

As it turned out, Marty Sklar was not right about the future. Years earlier, an openly Communist Ph.D. student of the great revolutionary-era historian Merrill Jensen had been turned down for his degree by the history department, which feared that giving him a doctorate at a time when Joseph McCarthy was the junior senator from the university's own state would do harm to the university. But the era of McCarthy, which would become so crucial to the worldview of the Left in years to come, was actually quite brief on the Madison campus. And despite my open affiliation and activity with the LYL, no avenues were ever closed to me. In fact, if I had remained on the left later on, my Communist past would probably have helped me rise in the ranks of academia. As it was, my gradual but public rejection of that past hurt my prospects.

Decades later, a book by Paul Buhle about Madison and the rise of the New Left not only glorified the activity of the Communist students of the 1950s, but, because I had begun to express my second thoughts, virtually read me out of its history entirely, in typical Soviet fashion. In *History and the New Left: Madison, Wisconsin, 1950–1970,* Buhle alludes to me anonymously as "a former ... Madison 'Red' now turned hysterical critic of the New Left," and then proceeds to give his readers scores of nostalgic remembrances from various of my former comrades, none of whom have had any shred of regret about their Communist past. I was informed by Marty Sklar, a continuing friend, that the letter Buhle sent around commissioning the pieces that comprise the book assured would-be contributors that I would not be included in the volume.

But I can now contribute my own, delayed recollections to that history. The first week on campus, I filled out a form declaring that I wanted to major in history. My assigned advisor was a new professor in the history department who had come from the State University of Iowa, a man named George Mosse. I knew little about him, although in fact Mosse was one of the world's most distinguished intellectual historians of Europe, Judaism and fascism. A son of the owner and publisher of the Mosse firm in Weimar Germany, George Mosse was able to escape the Holocaust because he was educated in Britain, and after Hitler's ascension to power, had decided to come to the United States. As both a student and a participant in the prewar European and German Left, Mosse was well prepared to deal with someone like myself, a precocious and highly opinionated know-it-all who thought he was making a contribution to world history by defending the Soviet Union.

Mosse suggested that I begin by taking his modern European history survey class, and since he was my advisor, he assigned me to his own discussion section, which was composed of upperclassmen and graduate students. Rather than be intimidated by people who were far better read than I was, I persisted in showing my ignorance with a great amount of arrogance. Thus I even condemned Arthur Koestler's *Invisible Writing* as a "worthless piece of anti-Soviet trash." I don't recall the reaction of my class-mates, many of whom went on to become top-notch historians specializing in European fascism, but Mosse loved my antics. He beamed as I spoke, happy to find someone here in America who resembled the kind of radical he had known in Europe. With-out the slightest bit of condescension, Mosse let me know that I had a lot to learn, and that in the future I might come to feel differently about Koestler and his observations. In the years to come, Mosse would remind me of my youthful persona many times, the last at a dinner in Washington, D.C., shortly before he passed away in 1998.

Mosse regularly shocked and impressed us in class. After Fidel Castro's rise to power in 1959, he dared to compare Castro's mass rallies to the hysterical public style of Mussolini in prewar Italy. We on the left had all become devotees and supporters of Castro, and we were outraged by the comparison. But Mosse's consistent willingness to engage us, debate with us and seek our friendship was disarming. He described us as a group who were really only "Marxists of the heart, Kantianizing Marxists with eth-ical imperatives."

As a freshman, I signed up for almost every history course I could take. As it turned out, Howard K. Beale, the distinguished historian and biographer of Theodore Roosevelt and an old Madison progressive, taught the U.S. history survey. My political mentor Marty Sklar led the discussion section for Beale's course, and hence I had the unique ability to combine my studies with my growing political role on campus. My growing friendship with Marty did not, however, interfere with his role as my instructor. He had taught me to regard the classroom and the university as equivalent to the proletarian's factory, and instilled in me the ethic that to be a good Communist, my first job was to excel in my studies.

I soon emerged as the campus spokesman for student Commu-nists. And we found that we had a big fight on our hands, not with students but with Madison residents, especially those who were members of the American Legion and had fought in either the Second World War or more recently in Korea. The *Badger Legionnaire,* a Legion publication, featured a special issue under the headline "The Situation at Madison ... Shelter for the LYL." But its call to suppress our league and the speakers it was bringing to campus only made our light shine even brighter; in fact, the Legion campaign made us local celebrities. We preened in our new role of defenders of civil liberties and academic freedom.

If all we had done was try to obtain a forum for the ideology of Marxism-Leninism, we might have been carrying out a valid intellectual function, that of promoting free debate in the marketplace of ideas. But in fact our objective was classically Leninist: to gain influence in, and if possible take over, other existing student groups. One of our "secret" members was a paunchy New Yorker named Jeff Kaplow, who admitted in Paul Buhle's book:

> If Madison in the 1950s was quasi-unique in being the only university community not to brand us young Reds as pariahs, we were nonetheless constrained to work quietly. There was no other choice but to work within the framework of other organizations whose aims were in some way compatible with our own. The words used to describe this activity—"infiltration" and "burrowing from within"—have an essentially negative connotation and are, as such, unjust. For we were not so much using those organizations for our own ends as we were helping them fulfill their stated aims.

So, by trying to take over other student organizations, we were merely helping them on the road to self-fulfillment; as if the groups we infiltrated—be it the NAACP, the Young Democrats, the Students for Democratic Action (youth arm of the fiercely anti-Communist ADA), the Film Society, the Student Council, the Student League for Industrial Democracy (a social-democratic group)—aimed to overthrow our capitalist democracy and replace it with a socialist revolution modeled on the USSR.

LYL membership at Madison was close to one hundred, certainly a miniscule portion of the students at a huge state university campus, but a significant number nonetheless, since our cadre were all committed activists who met in their own small units—"cells," our enemies called them—and plotted to alter campus political life. To give an example of our machinations: in late November of 1955, a story appeared in the university newspaper, the *Daily Cardinal,* noting that "a group of university student leaders is preparing an 'amicus-curiae' (friend of the court) brief in the Labor Youth League's (LYL) appeal of the Communist-front provisions of the McCarran Internal Security Act of 1950 to the Court of Appeals in Washington, D.C." The brief was quite significant, since in that era, very few liberal and non-Communist groups had been willing to intervene on behalf of the rights of Communists. Now, at a major university campus, it appeared that prominent student leaders were going to do just that by taking up the cause of the LYL, which had been required to register with the federal government.

A few days later, the *Cardinal* featured the full text of the brief under the banner headline, "Campus Leaders Oppose MacCarran [*sic*] Act." The statement endorsed President Harry S. Truman's veto of the act, which it called "the most terrible threat to freedom so far devised in America." The brief claimed that the concern of the student leaders was not with the fortunes of the LYL, but with the act's "impact on the vast majority of American youth who are not members of the Labor Youth League, who may disagree with its policies or who may never have even heard of the Labor Youth League." Who could disagree with that common-sense statement?

The amicus curiae brief ended by listing the names of eighteen student leaders who had backed it. But there was one problem with the petition: it was actually written by the LYL leadership, specifically by the president of the Young Democrats, who unbeknown to the other signatories was a secret LYL member. His standing encouraged some other genuine student leaders to sign, but of the eighteen original signatories, at least seven were league members and others were close fellow travelers. The old Commie tactic of "burrowing from within" really did work.

During my freshman year at Wisconsin the FBI began assembling a file on me, which I later obtained under provisions of the

Freedom of Information Act. The entry for April 27, 1956, correctly gives my name and academic status, identifies me as an officer of the LYL, and notes my approval for "Detcom tabbing," an FBI indentification for detaining a person in case of a national security emergency. Among the activities the bureau tracked was my distribution of the *Daily Worker.* Indeed, early in December of 1955, I went to the gates of the Oscar Mayer meat packing firm in Madison with Matt Chapperon, who had replaced Jerry Fiderer as the other open LYL officer. We attempted to give issues to workers who were contemplating strike action, but they ignored us. The company called the police, who ordered us into their cars and told us that we were on private property and had to desist. I was scared out of my wits, having convinced myself that the police would beat the living daylights out of us, in true fascist fashion. Instead, after confiscating the bundle of Communist newspapers, they told us to be on our way. I felt relieved, now that I had a perfect excuse for leaving without having to fulfill my revolutionary duty. The FBI report of this incident notes that the material we distributed was retained in the bureau's Milwaukee office, where for all I know it still sits in a dusty file cabinet.

The times were changing, and when Khrushchev made his famous 1956 revelation about Stalin, even our small group of campus Reds got rather fed up with the secrecy and the Leninist model of organization demanded by the Communist Party. By the time I was a senior, the same year that Madison graduate students began what became the preeminent New Left academic journal, *Studies on the Left,* the LYL cadre felt that we needed a broader and more open socialist organization, one that overtly stated its aims, had no secret membership cells, and could carry on the struggle for socialism on a more hospitable basis. After meeting with the editors of the new journal, we decided to dissolve the league and form a new group called the Wisconsin Socialist Club. On the Sunday before we made the announcement, while I was sitting in Saul Landau's living room listening to the weekly radio broadcast by Walter Winchell, we were stunned to hear the following, in Winchell's trademark crackling voice: "Flash: Madison, Wisconsin—In a secret meeting, the

Communist Labor Youth League has dissolved and announced its reformation under the guise of a new public group, the Wisconsin Socialist Club." This proved what some of us had occasionally suspected: that there was an informer in our group.

As to the facts spelled out in Khrushchev's secret 1956 report on Stalinism, all members of the LYL believed they were no doubt true; but not all of the Wisconsin Communists seemed to believe them. Along with Matt Chapperon, I received a visit from the two leading Wisconsin Communists, Fred Blair and Sig Eisencher, long-time apparatchiks who ran the party from its Milwaukee office. They came to inform us that the shocking Khrushchev report was a CIA fabrication. Pending other information, they told us, we should regard it as a provocation. At the time they told us this, I later found out, they had already met with members of the CPUSA's Central Committee in New York, where party chairman Eugene Dennis had read the report aloud—before its publication in the *New York Times*—and verified its validity. Many at that meeting, it has been reported, broke down in tears. But once the report was made public, the party instructed its local leadership to inform the rank and file that Khrushchev had made no such speech.

When Soviet tanks rolled into Hungary in November 1956, some of us got access to the frank reports by the Communist reporter Peter Freyer, whose coverage in the London *Daily Worker* made it clear that the Hungarian working class was rising up against its Communist masters, and that the only true revolution occurring was one by the people against the commissars. I recall discussing this earnestly with Marty Sklar, who told me that indeed it seemed to be a true people's rebellion against the Hungarian government, and if the working class opposed socialism, it was their mistake and they would have to live with it. I rejected his view of the event, and stood firm. In fact, while many others took this historical moment to leave the Movement's ranks, I actually joined the Communist Party USA as a full-fledged member.

Having led the LYL through all these years, I was an accepted leader. I rallied my own troops on the Madison campus, discussing with others how their work in various "mass" organizations was going. In addition, I attended statewide meetings held in the Milwaukee area, where comrades from shop and farm groups would give their reports. I no longer recall what momentous issues we discussed, but instead I remember the comic-opera nature of some of these sessions.

One memorable meeting was held at a large Wisconsin farm. To get there, we had to leave Milwaukee early in the morning, traveling like characters in a cheap spy novel: lying down under the back seat of the car, and twice pulling over to the side of a dirt road, where we squirmed on our bellies to another waiting car to resume the ride. After the third transfer, we arrived at a farmhouse whose exact location was not identified. To reach the house, we crawled through cornfields to foil the police agents we imagined to be trailing us. At the meeting, we were quickly informed that we could not talk, as wiretaps were suspected, and had to write our comments on a blackboard that was passed around and then erased. This was cumbersome, but at least we could report to the Central Committee that despite the repression and hard times from the revisionist assault, the party continued to function.

Marxism had opponents on the Madison campus, and I considered it my job to take them on. Among other events I engaged in while the LYL still existed was a series of debates with those opponents. One of the most memorable of my public debates was against Bertell Ollman, a political science student who was then chairman of the Student League for Industrial Democracy, a group that brought Norman Thomas to campus, and which we regarded as a counterrevolutionary body. In the debate, I defended the "science" of Marxism and pointed to the great successes of the socialist world, led by the USSR—which Ollman, in turn, portrayed as a dictatorial regime that prevented real democracy. And of course, Ollman condemned us as apologists for totalitarianism.

Years later, in 1968, I bumped into Ollman again in the halls of the United Nations, where I had come to hear the delegates debate the Soviet invasion of Czechoslovakia. I approached him as the debate ended, not having seen him since we all had left Wisconsin. "Bertell," I said, "I apologize to you for all the nonsense I plied in our many debates. You were all too right, and I was wrong." Ollman responded, much to my shock, "No, Ron, you were right and I was wrong. Our task is to build the socialist revolution." The only social democrat in Madison had transformed himself into the stereotype of a revolutionary intellectual, while I, the former campus Commie, was now a bumbling social democrat!

History produces ironic outcomes. Bertell Ollman would gain notoriety as an extremely radical professor at New York University. He would also become famous in the 1970s as the author of a board game, "Class Struggle," designed to teach young people the principles of Marxist socialism through a parody of Parker Brothers' "Monopoly." Ollman's game sold like wildfire in New York, where it was featured in full-page ads by the luxurious Bloomingdale's chain in the pages of the *New York Times*. This success led him to write his autobiography, which was purchased by Hollywood.

College, of course, was not all classwork and politics. I did have a personal life, much of it spent with my first girlfriend. I spotted her attending one of our weekly folk sings and thought she was cute. "Cookie," as her friends called her, was a Wisconsin native and an ardent Zionist who regularly frequented Hillel, supported what I considered right-wing Labor Zionism, and danced in the Israeli folk dance group. She was disgusted by my Communist politics, but wrote them off as "adolescent rebellion against parental authorities." (Never mind that my parents were leftists, too.) Nevertheless, we enjoyed each other's company, and for almost two years we were inseparable. She said repeatedly that she was amazed to find that I didn't have horns, which is how she had always thought of American Reds. But nothing I said could sway her opposition to my views, and however much I liked her, I certainly wasn't going to become permanently committed to someone who did not share my worldview.

There were also renewed friendships, especially with two people I had known in New York: Eric Weissberg, who had been one of my bunkmates at Woodland; and Marshall Brickman, known in the Washington Square folk music scene as one of the best young bluegrass banjo pickers around. Marshall also came from a bona fide Red-diaper-baby family. When Marshall and Eric arrived in Madison, we took an off-campus apartment I had obtained along with Matt Chapperon. Matt was highly political and sectarian, always concerned with developing the right Marxist position on music and other subjects. Marshall and Eric, although certainly considering themselves part of the Left community, were relatively nonpolitical, and concerned mainly with developing their expertise on the banjo. Together they would spend hours a day slowing down LP records and precisely diagramming the banjo breaks played by Earl Scruggs. I was in awe of their musicianship, but I strained our relationship by insisting on playing with them publicly, despite the fact that my Seeger-style song leading was amateurish in comparison with their playing. Once, after much insistence on my part, Marshall and Eric allowed me to work up three songs with them, which we performed in Chicago at the Gate of Horn as part of Theodore Bikel's radio show, broadcast live from its stage.

Besides trying to compete with them musically, I spent a fair amount of time discussing personal affairs and politics particularly with Marshall, who was then, and still is, an extremely witty and brilliant individual. Marshall never joined any of our political groups, a decision for which I constantly criticized him at the time. But we had much in common, such as having to serve in the compulsory campus ROTC program. Nothing could have been more foreign to me as a budding young Communist than having to put on an Air Force uniform three times a week, go to ROTC class, and attend weekly drills, which I never could master. It was bad enough having to march in the annual Armed Forces Day parade with my unit, but the last straw was the final exam. The test involved discussing the strategy of bombing raids. We were asked to "list the advantages of having U.S. bases overseas," and to write an essay on how one might prepare to engage in a bombing run over the Soviet Union. I responded to the latter by writing simply, "I wouldn't," and as for the advantages of overseas air bases, "there are none." Not surprisingly, I received a grade of F, as did Marshall. We both were ordered to take the ROTC course again the next year.

Marshall also responded by writing the sketches for our alternative to the annual Military Ball, which ROTC cadets from the
different services attended in full uniform with their dates. We
called our affair the "Anti-Military Ball," and it was perhaps the
first example of a countercultural event on the Wisconsin campus. Brickman's skill as a humorist would express itself years later
when he collaborated with Woody Allen in the writing of *Annie
Hall* and other films. In those years, atomic testing and radioac-
tivity were key issues of the still young peace movement, and
Brickman wrote a skit he called "To Boom or Not to Boom: A
Twentieth-Century Hamlet," or "All Out for Fallout." Because of
his wit, attendance at the Anti-Military Ball grew from year to
year.

Although I considered Marshall one of my best friends, we
had a stormy relationship because I was already putting him
down for not being true to his Marxist principles, and I badg-
ered him about his excessively cultural interests. I was envious
when his parents, good Communists themselves, bought him a
ticket to attend the World Youth Festival in the USSR, while I
who desperately wanted to go didn't have the money to travel to
the socialist wonderland. My parents, seeking to protect me from
too-close contact with the Communist Party, simply refused to
finance the trip. After Marshall returned from the USSR, the FBI
appeared regularly at our front door, and once even accosted
him as he entered his French class.

In New York during spring vacation, I threw a party for Marshall at my parents' apartment, where he showed his slides from
the USSR and spoke about his experience. The high of going to
Moscow as an honored guest even led him to abandon his usually cynical attitude towards politics. I recall him showing a picture of a cop in white uniform directing traffic near Red Square,
and commenting that this proved how ridiculous was the claim
that the USSR was a police state. Virtually the cream of the New
York LYL showed up for the party, and my stock in the Movement rose considerably. My parents, however, noticed something
afterward that made them none too happy: One of the young
comrades evidently had seen fit to carve a hammer and sickle
into the stone of a modernist Mexican lamp that they proudly

displayed in their living room. This loving act of revolutionary solidarity ruined the lamp and considerably lowered its value.

I convinced Marshall to get a job with me at Bronx House Camp where I had decided to return for the summer of 1958. He agreed, and we decided to purchase a used car together— a foolish move, given that I didn't know how to drive. Unfortunately, the car lasted only a few weeks; Marshall lent it to another counselor, who got drunk and cracked it up beyond repair. I was so angry that I didn't speak to him for weeks.

That same summer, I met a young high school student who within a year would become my wife. Four years younger than me, Alice Schweig was assigned to work as a junior counselor in the young children's camp, in which I was a senior counselor. Alice was a tall, good-looking girl. We were deeply attracted to each other, and within the first week of camp, we had paired off. At summer's end, I returned to Wisconsin while she went back to her high school, but we kept up our relationship. We wrote daily, sometimes two or three times a day, and met a few times during the school year. Once, she flew to Chicago, where we spent a night at a friend's apartment, and then drove on to Washington, D.C., to attend an event called the Youth March for Civil Rights, led by Bayard Rustin, Martin Luther King Jr., and Michael Harrington; this was a little-known precursor to the great 1963 March on Washington.

By the next summer (1959), when Alice was ready to begin college and I was headed for graduate school, we made the decision to get married. My letters reveal that I put a great deal of pressure on her, imploring her to understand that our love for each other meant that we were bound to be together, and that it was foolhardy to let a little thing like college stand in the way. It seems incredible that our parents let us go through with the marriage. She was barely eighteen and I was twenty-one; we were both young, naïve, without any means of earning a living—and sure that none of this mattered. Alice applied to the State University of Iowa, the school I had decided to attend since they had given me a scholarship to earn my master's degree. With a part-time job in addition to my grant, I assured her parents that we could make it, especially if they continued to support her in the way they had originally planned.

It was easy getting Alice to adopt my political worldview. Growing up as a solitary Jew in what was then an all-WASP Westchester suburb of Pelham, the only area in New York State that would vote solidly for Barry Goldwater, Alice had felt something of an alien. Granted, her father was a wealthy and well-known pediatrician, a man of immense charm and good looks, who had as his friends some of the most prominent artists, writers and cultural figures in New York. But one day, as Alice and I looked through the attic in her parents' home, I found well-preserved copies of Communist books, magazines and literature, all conveniently stored away to be out of sight during the McCarthy period. I surmised, correctly as it turned out, that her parents had been in the Communist orbit, and although no longer open about it, they would not look askance at a partner for Alice who was committed to the dreams and hopes of their own left-wing youth. Our romance was bound up with the fortunes of the Movement, and we were excited at the beginning of our journey through the future.

The summer before we went off to Iowa, Alice and I both worked at the leading Communist Party summer camp, once called Camp Unity but now changed to the more innocuous Wingdale on the Lake. Wingdale was not a children's camp, but rather an adult resort for party members, their families, and other fellow travelers. It had a well-earned reputation as a den of free love, a place where uptight apparatchiks abandoned all pretenses and let their libidos loose. In particular, the adult female campers seemed to indulge in behavior that was never openly acknowledged or condoned, but appeared to be the favored sexual activity of the camp: sex with black male staff and campers, which could not be condemned because of the party's ongoing campaign against "white chauvinism." It was also the first I had ever heard of group sex and swapping, with the highly prized black lifeguard and his white roommate regularly switching partners as part of their camp routine.

Alice was a waitress at the camp, and worked hard in the kitchen for her three meals a day. I had been hired as the folk-music leader, which involved little more than leading songs at the campfire once a week and being MC at the Saturday night shows. I also presided over the guests who came to speak and lead educational sessions at the camp. Once we had Ben Davis, the famed Communist Party leader from Harlem; another time it was Harry Magdoff, later editor of the so-called "independent socialist" *Monthly Review* and a leading Maoist, but at the time very close to the Communist Party. Another prominent guest was Lorraine Hansberry, who achieved stardom that summer when her play *Raisin in the Sun* was accepted for a Broadway run.

Alice and I were married in the summer of 1959 at the home her family had in the Adirondacks. It was set majestically on a series of rocks on the banks of Indian Lake, one of the magnificent, untouched waterways in the mountains. A log house with huge wood beams, built in the 1930s, it looked like one of the old country houses of the rich from the pre-Depression era. It was filled with a few of our best friends, and the family and friends of our parents. The wedding was on Labor Day weekend, and after the ceremony we drove into New York to spend one night in town. We celebrated our wedding by watching the annual proletarian Labor Day parade that still marched through downtown New York.

Towards a New Left

MOVING TO IOWA, WHICH SOME PEOPLE INSISTED ON REFERRING to as "the rectum of the Midwest," was indeed a shock. Freezing in the wintertime, Iowa City boasted one small, dilapidated movie theater, many bars, few restaurants, and water so undrinkable that even in those environmentally unenlightened times the state warned citizens to drink only bottled water. Yet the town also had its bohemian and political fringe, much of it in the famed Writers' Workshop at the State University of Iowa, where brilliant young authors received training from major literary figures.

One of the workshop members was a young poet named Bob Mezey, who later would be heralded as America's poet laureate by none other than T. S. Eliot. Mezey, it turned out, was also a master guitar picker and folk singer, whose expertise was in the dazzling fingerpicking style of guitar developed by Merle Travis. He could often be found in what was the university's first off-campus, Greenwich Village–style coffee shop, where we would often hang out, pick and sing, and find others who shared our left-wing political views.

Another person who turned up was to become a lifelong friend and associate, Sol Stern—later to be one of the key editors of *Ramparts* along with Bob Scheer and Warren Hinckle in its radical heyday, and much later to be the journalist with whom I started my research on the Rosenberg case. Sol was another New York Jew who had attended the City College of New York (CCNY), and had been active in its left-wing milieu. Sol, however, was already a confirmed and cynical anti-Stalinist who regularly ridiculed my orthodoxy, although sharing my basic socialist assumptions. Together with my wife, we decided to create the same kind of political presence that we had built in Madison. We formed the Iowa Socialist Discussion Club, and quickly announced a schedule of meetings and events.

Much to our amazement, the SDC took off. With hardly a drop of effort, we attracted whatever mavericks, radical graduate students, carefully hidden Stalinists and assorted peaceniks existed in Iowa City at the start of the 1960s. My faculty advisor was a noted historian of the Progressive Era, Samuel P. Hays, who as it turned out was an authentic Quaker pacifist with ties to the yet small peace movement. In no way a socialist, Hays, because of his peace orientation, had ties to radicals and the new civil rights movement. A faculty member who taught French history, Alan Spitzer, was clearly a Marxist, and the professor who taught German history, Richard M. Hunt, was a left-wing anti-Communist socialist. In those days, their socialist views were expressed only in their scholarship, and they did not seek to recruit or indoctrinate their students. Even so, they made us feel we were really not isolated.

Our sympathies were aroused by the activity in the South undertaken by the Student Non-Violent Coordinating Committee, or SNCC. We understood that our part in the North was to join in acts of solidarity with the black students who were being arrested for asserting their rights in the heartland of the Old South. In a letter my wife and I wrote to the Iowa campus newspaper, we proposed that Iowans join the recently announced national boycott of the Woolworth and Kresge chain stores, which had refused to rescind the directives prohibiting their southern branches from serving blacks. We pointed to the example set by a picket line of five hundred protestors in New York City, as well as smaller ones at Cornell and Rutgers universities.

Although I privately believed that the struggle against segregation was part of the broader struggle for socialism, I had not mentioned this in our letter, focusing instead on fulfilling the promise of American democracy. It was good Popular Front–era politics, in which those who had joined in could be approached later in the struggle to participate in the revolutionary vanguard. Unfortunately, a local paper checked into my past in Madison and uncovered my Communist affiliations. The result was a spate of phone calls threatening Alice and me with violence and demanding that we call the protest off. Still we persisted, and during a sunny Saturday lunch hour in late March of 1960, ninety of us gathered to form a picket line in support of the Woolworth and Kresge boycott—evidently an unprecedented event for tiny Iowa City. Hecklers appeared en masse, and Joel Silbey, a graduate student and decades later an eminent Cornell University political historian, was spat on by the march's opponents.

After this, we concentrated on organizing the Socialist Discussion Club. With an Iowa vet and former Trotskyist named Thomas Jerry Barret, we formed the group's executive board and worked to schedule meetings and gain recruits. As we put it in the campus newspaper, we wanted to "become an effective center for those who question the drift of the U.S. power elite to war," and to push for an alternative "planned economy" not based on profit from war and destruction. Our second goal was to gain understanding and support for "the Marxist-Socialist viewpoint" on campus through "the exchange of ideas of a socialist nature." We even succeeded in recruiting a few young idealist Iowa natives. One of our active members was a young student named Ed Mezvinsky, who came from one of the prominent and fairly well-off Jewish families in Iowa. Later, Mezvinsky would become a household name as the congressman from Iowa who held a seat on the House Watergate committee, and who spoke out often during the Nixon impeachment hearings.

The year at Iowa went all too quickly. Learning to live in a new marriage, staying in the library each night until 1 or 2 A.M., and working in the civil rights movement made up my life. I decided to write my master's thesis, a required step towards getting a Ph.D., on Henry A. Wallace, the left-wing vice president under Franklin Roosevelt and secretary of commerce under Truman, who achieved fame in the Left as the only prominent political figure willing to buck Truman's Cold War and anti-Soviet foreign policy. Wallace was viewed as a radical when he ran for president in 1948, but I treated him as a conservative who sought to attain an international balance of power, while obtaining new markets abroad for American business as the pathway toward world peace.

As part of my work I arranged a visit with Wallace, who received me at his South Salem, New York, farm during my spring break. I even got an audience with President Truman as well, at his library office in Independence, Missouri. I was so naïve, I didn't know that one referred to the nation's former chief executive as "Mr. President," and I rankled the library's director by calling him "Mr. Truman." Still, President Truman talked with me for over an hour, answering my questions and chatting amiably about his views of Wallace and the Cold War.

Meeting Henry Wallace, it turned out, was far more exciting. He was, of course, one of the heroes of the Old Left, a man who may have supported the Korean War and deserted the ranks of the Progressive Party, yet was still remembered as America's last great hope for achieving a modus vivendi with Joe Stalin. I arrived at South Salem by train from New York's Grand Central Station and looked for Wallace at the platform, where he said he would be waiting. I saw him standing in front of a Lincoln Continental sedan parked nearby. I introduced myself, shook his hand, and walked towards the Lincoln; but Wallace, notorious for his thrift, said, "No, not that car," and took me instead to a Volkswagen Bug! And then the former vice president of the United States drove me at eighty miles an hour down country roads to his sprawling South Salem farm, while I held on to the door handle for dear life.

For the rest of the long day, Wallace was warm and anxious to help a novice graduate student, freely answering all my long and involved questions. He also gave me free access to his unpublished diaries, which others would not see for years. I was able to look up particular entries, take notes, and if other questions came up later, write to him and get his responses. Wallace and his wife also offered me a home-cooked lunch. At the day's end, he took me to his chicken farm. Always something of the mad scientist, he had been breeding an all-white-meat chicken whose hens mysteriously laid green eggs. He carefully gathered a dozen of the green eggs in a carton, which I proudly took home to my mother. Looking at them, she said, "I'm not using any eggs that are green, even if Henry Wallace gave them to you." With that she threw them in the garbage! I have often wondered whether, if Wallace had still been part of the pro-Stalinist Left, she would have given them a try.

In September of 1961, I returned to Madison with a master's degree from Iowa, to begin working toward my doctorate in history. The lure was to work with William Appleman Williams, a historian whose intelligence and charisma affected everyone he touched. Hailing from the small town of Atlantic, Iowa (once he and I were walking through Macy's Department Store in New York City when Bill quipped that his entire town could fit in the store's basement), Williams graduated from the U.S. Naval Academy in Annapolis, and suffered major injuries when the ship he served on was torpedoed during World War II. He was a unique figure, an authentic American radical, whose own brand of socialism combined the nationalist neo-isolationism of Charles A. Beard with the Progressive reform impulse of Teddy Roosevelt and Woodrow Wilson, and with the desire for community that drove Eugene V. Debs.

Williams was generally regarded as the dean of the Cold War revisionists, historians who argued that the nature of the American expansionist system led its postwar leaders to initiate what became the Cold War with the Soviet Union. With the publication of *The Tragedy of American Diplomacy* in 1959, Williams became a major intellectual influence, particularly after A. A. Berle Jr. reviewed his book favorably in the pages of the *New York Times Book Review*. That the former New Dealer who would soon become assistant secretary of state for Latin American affairs in the Kennedy administration looked favorably upon Williams' worldview spoke well for him, and it meant that his critique of the United States would be taken seriously. Not only did it gain the attention of a new generation of historians and scholars, but more importantly *The Tragedy of American Diplomacy* became a sacred text for a new generation of activists and students who were seeking an intellectual rationale for their gut-level animosity to the postwar American culture. Eventually, Williams chose to leave Madison because the New Left had become so intransigent that it even turned against his own kind of moderate radicalism. In the heyday of 1960s activism, a group of New Left students stormed his lecture wearing gorilla suits and handing out bananas, in response to a *New York Times* story that quoted him as calling New Leftists a bunch of "apes."

Williams held that the American reluctance to sympathize with revolution abroad stemmed from the ideology of the Open Door, proclaimed first by Secretary of State John Hay in the Open Door Notes of 1898–99. This policy, Williams argued, defined the nation's never-ending search for foreign markets, a quest that led to the creation of a new kind of empire practicing an anti-imperialistic imperialism. "The history of the Open Door Notes," Williams wrote, "became the history of American foreign relations."

Williams' argument was brilliant, but fatally flawed by his view of the Soviet Union as a harmless power, a weak and vanquished nation that was incapable of promoting any international mischief, not to speak of harboring expansionist aims. As he wrote in 1978 in *America in a Changing World,* "the Cold War could probably have been avoided if the United States had either accepted Russian predominance in Eastern Europe or had used its economic power to negotiate Russian withdrawal in return for help in reconstruction and a mutual security alliance." The U.S. did not take this path, Williams continued, because it "desired to apply the ideological and economic principles of the Open Door policy in Eastern Europe," and hence used its power in an anti-Soviet fashion. Stalin, Williams implied, was simply a benign nationalist who only sought stability within his own sphere of influence.

Since Williams wrote those words, of course, the Soviet Union has collapsed and new material in the former Soviet archives has confirmed what old Cold Warriors always knew—that as the historian John L. Gaddis has put it, Stalin was responsible for the Cold War, and given his goals and agenda, it was inevitable.

Williams applied the same logic to Castro's Cuba, also. In *The United States, Cuba and Castro* (1962), he argued that Castro, as an honest revolutionary, had no choice but to break the binding ties with the informal American empire which had existed since the end of the Spanish-American War, if he were to honor the promises that had been made but never kept by Fulgencio Batista in the 1952 Cuban Constitution. As for Castro's turning to the Soviet Union for aid, that too was the fault of the United States. "By giving up on Castro and becoming increasingly negative and antagonistic," Williams wrote, "the United States closed off the one main chance Castro had to make his revolution without turning to the Communists in Cuba and the Soviet Union."

That argument would be repeated over and over through the years by scores of leftists, who used Williams' ideas to justify their belief that Castro was forced into the arms of the Soviets by an American foreign policy opposed to allowing peoples to exercise what Williams called "the right of revolution."

To support his position, Williams indulged in the same kind of tortured logic that other fellow travelers used to justify Stalin's repression. At the revolution's start, Castro arrested and imprisoned the general and fellow revolutionary Huber Matos, who served twenty-five years for treason, much of it in solitary confinement. Matos was a leader of the rebel army in Camaguey province, who from the start worried about growing Communist influence in the Castro camp. He finally submitted his resignation to Castro, and soon was arrested and put on trial. Williams wrote that Castro's charge of treason was correct, since "Matos was resigning and taking with him a nucleus of trained military officers and experienced political leaders." Acknowledging that by American standards of justice, perhaps, "Matos had not committed treason," Williams then argued that by Cuban standards, he was in essence guilty of "the common definition of treason," being "action considered inimical to the existing state."

Those of us who followed Williams ignored his poorly reasoned apologia. When we tried to lead a campus protest against the Bay of Pigs invasion, our inspiration was Williams, who had taught us that all Castro was guilty of was trying to free his people from the control of the American empire. Williams was strangely oblivious to the oppression foisted upon the peoples under Soviet hegemony; he seemed only concerned with U.S. policy toward the Soviet bloc, which he thought was centered on thwarting just and necessary social revolutions. It is true that

HUAC and local superpatriots ignored the bravery and commitment of his service to the nation during World War II when they went after him. Williams traveled under subpoena to Washington, D.C., only to find that HUAC, having been warned about his war record and his reputation, decided to quash his subpoena. The local equivalent HUAC, an investigating body in the state legislature, was not so considerate, but queried him about what he taught in a public hearing. Williams responded, "I teach students how to think." Then he baited them by quoting American documents about the "right of revolution." From the galleries, we all cheered.

We also were pleased that Williams showed nothing but disdain for the old, sectarian, pro-Communist left wing, from which we believed ourselves to have graduated into a New Left. He may have given the Soviets the benefit of the doubt in his analysis of the Cold War, yet he had no love for their American apologists, whether of the Stalinist, Trotskyist, or "independent socialist" variety. Williams would provoke the Old Left spokesmen to anger on a regular basis. When the Communist Party's leading intellectual, the historian Herbert Aptheker, came to speak under the sponsorship of our Wisconsin Socialist Club, he attacked Williams, condemning his sympathy for Charles Beard and his supposed warmness toward pre–World War II isolationism.

The next day, when Aptheker appeared at his office for a social call, Williams met him at the door, looked him up and down, and said, "These aren't my office hours. Come back next week." Then he closed the door in Aptheker's face. The next week, Aptheker actually flew back from New York to arrive for Williams' office hours. When he walked in, Williams said, "I'm not interested in talking to you." Aptheker turned abruptly and left.

With Williams as our guide and inspiration, we decided to produce a new journal of ideas to capture the excitement of the revisionist thinking that would be part of the New Left. We all shared what historian and founding editor James Weinstein called "an awareness of the severe failure of the old left, and a commitment

to participate in the development of a body of theory to stimu-
late the creation of a new revolutionary movement in the United
States," by trying to develop "socialist thought" that would take
American reality into account.

Studies on the Left (or *Studies,* as we usually called it) aimed to
create a theoretical basis for a new radical movement. Its main
contribution, which I played a small part in formulating, was a
theory about "corporate liberalism." In its sophisticated form, it
claimed that the dominant worldview of American political leaders was not one of laissez faire, but rather a managerial form of
liberalism that invisibly molded the various civic groups composing American society into consensus, thereby eliminating real
dissent.

In its cruder form, the theory of corporate liberalism was used
to argue that in the United States, the true enemy of the Left was
not the "reactionaries," i.e., old-style Republicans and conservatives, but rather the liberals who comprised what they liked to
call the "vital center." Later on, when the New Left was on a war
footing, the theory was reduced to a slogan: "Liberals and liberalism are the enemy." For the group around *Studies on the Left,*
the target was not those who had truly reactionary positions—
out-and-out racists, for example—but rather those who considered themselves practical, realistic and moderate, who didn't
dream of building a revolutionary utopia.

For instance, when the civil rights leader Bayard Rustin wrote
the influential essay "From Protest to Politics" for *Commentary*
magazine (February 1965), calling for a "coalition strategy," an
alliance of American blacks with liberals and the labor movement to produce a majority movement on behalf of civil rights
and formal political equality, he became the enemy. I wrote an
essay accusing Rustin of directing the movement "into cooperation with the dominant system of oppression." This article was
first printed in a mimeographed newsletter called *Freedom North,*
an adjunct of the Student Non-Violent Coordinating Committee, and later appeared in a book called *The Great Society Reader:
The Failure of American Liberalism.* The "Negro rebellion," I
asserted, "must evolve to a revolutionary position." The heart of
my argument was the claim that those who wanted coalition

politics—like Rustin—were being used by the Johnson administration, which wanted "the Negro movement tied to the corporate system."

As a result of my attack, I was invited to address Ella Baker,
the "Grandmother of SNCC," and an assorted group of the
Southern SNCC leadership, at a conference held in Nyack, New
York. There, I repeated my attack on Rustin to a friendly group,
who found in my argument theoretical justification for their
growing move away from Martin Luther King Jr. to "Black Power"
and black nationalism. Rustin, I arrogantly concluded, was not
a civil rights leader, but a theoretician of "moderate white liberals who fear radical change and of the administration that con-
tinues to play politics at home and wage war abroad."

Many years later, in the late 1970s, I finally met Rustin at a
party thrown by Martin Luther King Jr.'s biographer, David Gar-
row. "Bayard," I said, "I'm the guy who condemned you so
thoughtlessly years ago, and who accused you of selling out the
struggle. I just wanted you to know that I realize you were right,
and I apologize." Rustin laughed heartily. "Don't worry," he
responded. "When A. Philip Randolph [Rustin's mentor and the
founder of the March on Washington movement] called off his
threatened antidraft movement in 1940, I called him a fascist
sellout."

I also did my part to popularize the *Studies* viewpoint among
the ranks of the Old Left by writing a long article for the so-
called "independent socialist" magazine *Monthly Review,* edited
by Paul M. Sweezy and Leo Huberman, two old-line, pro-Soviet
Marxists who had minor differences with the tactics and orga-
nizational demands of the official American Communist Party.
I hoped that I could explain to them why we were on their side,
and how our theoretical breakthrough was worthy of their understanding, if not their active support. My article was published in
their February 1963 issue under the title "American Radicalism:
Liberal or Socialist?" The gist was that the Old Left might have
supported reform, but in fact had not undertaken a "fundamental criticism of the capitalist system." My immediate target
was the ideology propagated by American Communists, who
called for unity against the so-called "ultra-Right," by which they

meant the Goldwater Republicans, and a united front with liberals to defeat them. The heart of the article was based on the
work of William Appleman Williams' disciples, who argued that
even the best of American liberalism, such as FDR's New Deal,
was nothing but a new way to pursue the traditional American
policy of seeking frontiers abroad.

My concern was that the New Left present its own revolutionary alternative to the corporate system, and not repeat the
wartime policy of the Communist Party, which had beat the
drums for FDR and was nothing but a left-wing adjunct of his
New Deal. I described all liberal leaders, from Henry A. Wallace
to John F. Kennedy, as supporters of the Open Door, Williams'
code word for support of American imperial hegemony over the
world. Radicals, I said, had to "dispense with liberalism" and
boldly proclaim socialism as the only alternative. It was liberals
who had developed the idea that communism had to be
opposed. Hence the real threat to humanity lay within the
United States, and emanated from the corporate liberal leaders.

Although intellectually rather crude, this article created a
small storm in the ranks of the Old Left. *Monthly Review* was
inundated with mail. I found myself accused of "anti-
Communism" because I had pointed out that the only thing dif-
ferentiating the Communists from FDR supporters was their
support of the Soviet Union. "Like ice cream," one reader wrote,
"anti-Communism ... comes in many flavors." Soon after, the
official Communist Party joined in, denouncing what it called
"the Radosh tendency on the Left."

Our ideas had consequences. When *Studies on the Left* moved
its offices to New York City in 1963, one former student radical
who joined the board was a very young Tom Hayden. Eventually,
while the original *Studies* editors wanted a new Left that would
develop a "revolutionary socialist consciousness," Hayden and
his supporters wanted an issues-driven activism, with stylistic mil-
itancy defining the essence of radicalism. The new group emphasized community organizing, student work on behalf of the poor,
and less attention to what it considered purely academic and theoretical concerns. It was what Irving Howe, in the first devastat-
ing criticism of the New Left ever written, was to call "New Styles

in Leftism." And when SDS held its first March on Washington in April 1965, the issue of communism and its relation to the New Left arose once again. SDS invited all groups opposed to the war to participate, including members of the old-line Communist and Trotskyist organizations. When Irving Howe and other democratic socialists demanded that any antiwar group they joined must renounce all forms of totalitarianism and exclude its American domestic supporters, *Studies* joined SDS in condemning their opposition as "Red-baiting." The new peace movement was one that viewed the United States, in James Weinstein's terms, "as the leading imperialist power in the world," devoted to a neocolonialism that was camouflaged "behind the ideology of anti-communism." As Staughton Lynd and Tom Hayden would proclaim in the journal's pages, anticommunism was "the moral equivalent of rape."

In Madison, Alice and I lived in a studio apartment off the main drag, State Street, rented from a rigid athletics teacher who demanded total quiet. My intellectual life was exciting; my married life involved constant bickering and fighting. I repressed the thought that we never should have married in the first place by throwing myself into what we were beginning to call "the Movement," and into folk music.

One day, a young kid, very thin but with traces of baby fat on him, came knocking at our door, carrying a guitar and little else. He appeared to be just coming out of innocence. He had got my name, he said, from Carl Granich, Michael Gold's son, who was a friend and awesome guitar picker from the young Communist circle in New York City. He had just arrived in Madison by bus. "I need a place to stay," he said. "Can you put me up?" With only one room, this was not possible, so I sent the kid—his name was Bob Dylan, he told me—to the apartment shared by my friends Paul Breines and Danny Kalb on Mifflin Street (later to become the Wisconsin equivalent of Berkeley's Telegraph Avenue). Bobby stayed for a few weeks, a stopover before he set out to find Woody Guthrie in New York.

It seemed to me that Dylan was a young Woody Guthrie: he sounded and played like Woody, and wore a workingman's cap that he had copied from one Guthrie wore in a famous picture. As he acknowledged in an interview years later, he was a "virtual Woody Guthrie jukebox." Bob would come out to join us on spring afternoons on the Student Union terrace, where we would sit on the lawn, look at the girls, and intermittently pick and sing. One day we got into the ultimate "what are you going to do when you grow up" conversation. Dylan looked at me earnestly and said, with a tone of complete assurance, "I'm going to be as big a star as Elvis Presley." I recall giving him a rather skeptical response, but Bob responded, "No, you'll see. I'll play the same and even bigger arenas. I know it."

Once, Dylan showed up at one of the regular parties our crowd regularly held on weekends. As usual, he took out his guitar and started to play. Other people, however, preferred talking politics, socializing and dancing. Finally, our friend Freddy Ciporen, then a Socialist Club stalwart and now a major New York publisher, got angry. He walked over to Dylan and said harshly, "Bob, would you put that damn guitar away already? Nobody wants to hear you anymore!" Dylan sheepishly got up and stashed the guitar back into its case. Soon, he got a ride back to New York with some friends.

A few months later, I was sitting on the university Terrace when I saw a smiling Dylan approaching me. "I'm back," he proudly said. "I got to New York, saw Woody and met a lot of people." Dylan announced he was going to stay for a while longer, before he was ready to move on for good. I gave him the schedule of upcoming folk events. At the time, we had regular, impromptu "hootenanny" sessions in a small new café on State Street, a place modeled on Greenwich Village hangouts. We all took our turns picking and singing. I recall performing a very sectarian ballad written by Irwin Silber of People's Songs, "Talkin' Un-American Blues," an attack on HUAC written in the style Woody used in so many of his own talking blues. Dylan watched me sing it and said, "That was great! That song really says something." He then picked up his guitar, and I recall that we sang a few Guthrie songs including "New York Town." In the years to come, I often wished someone had been running a tape recorder at these regular sessions.

The second year back in Wisconsin, Alice and I moved from our small studio apartment back to the roomy place I had rented with Marshall Brickman and Eric Weissberg during my senior year. It had three bedrooms, and we were able to rent one of them out to a tenant, which helped with our payments. In February of 1963, our first child, Laura, was born. Alice was in her last year of college, and I was finishing the required coursework and tests for the Ph.D. Because of our flexible schedule, we were somehow able to fit in child rearing and still get to class, work and even have a social life. Our best friends at the time were Paul Breines and his girlfriend and later wife, Wini Jacoby.

Others in our crowd included Saul and Nina Landau, whom I had already known as an undergraduate. Saul had become the founder of the Fair Play for Cuba youth group after the 1959 revolution, and had begun running trips to Cuba to show off the revolution. In the years ahead, Saul would become perhaps America's most ardent Castro admirer, PR representative, and sycophantic supporter. He made two different documentary films about Castro, the first one in the early 1960s, called *Fidel.* He had been taught how to use the camera during his trips to Cuba by the legendary Cuban cinematographer and later dissident exile and Oscar winner, Nestor Almendros. Nestor once told me, shortly before his death in the 1980s, that his one great regret was that he ever taught Saul Landau anything about filmmaking.

About this time, as a historian and would-be intellectual, I became very impressed with the writings of the Polish Marxist historian Isaac Deutscher, who would become a biographer of Leon Trotsky and would develop a unique outlook on the Soviet Union. Deutscher provided a convenient way for those who had been enamored with the USSR and Stalin to remain loyal to the ideal of communism while being critical of the reality. Contrary to Trotsky, who thought that the Soviet Union had become a "deformed worker's state," Deutscher viewed it as an authentic socialist society, whose population had now moved to the point where it could discard the residue of Stalinism and create a socialism more akin to the original Marxist ideal.

Deutscher told the truth about Stalin's reign, and his revelations about Soviet policy were eye-openers to those of us who had been blinded by lies for so long. As an orthodox Trotskyist quipped, for those infatuated with Stalinism, he was a bridge away from it; for those who were already anti-Stalinist, he was a bridge toward acceptance of it. I fit into the former group. Paul Breines and I awaited every publication written by Deutscher, and read each with a sense that we were finding the truth for the first time. I brought Deutscher to the attention of the *Studies* board, which at first, because of the editors' own Stalinist background, was dubious about him. But I gave them his articles, and as a result, they invited him to contribute to the journal.

My infatuation with the writings of Deutscher brought me further trouble with the Communist movement. One time, the party sent its top youth organizer, Danny Rubin, to stay with us. Looking at our bookshelves, Rubin spotted the Isaac Deutscher books and threw a fit. "As a good Communist," he said in a voice filled with anger and disgust, "you cannot read this junk. Get rid of it!" Then, he pulled out a copy of the monthly journal of the Communist Information Bureau, successor to the Comintern, called *World Marxist Review.* "This is what you should be reading, not Trotskyite junk." This small episode shocked me. Suddenly, I saw what had turned Budd Schulberg around after the party denounced his novel *What Made Sammy Run?* and demanded changes in the manuscript. I realized what humiliation the Hollywood Communist screenwriter Albert Maltz had suffered after the party forced him to recant a favorable review he had given to a novel by the then Trotskyist author James T. Farrell. True, the times were different now, and this was on a much smaller scale. But it was the same mentality on display, and as a young man of vast intellectual curiosity, I was beginning to discern the true face of Stalinism. Danny Rubin's admonition came as a rude awakening.

Laura was a very easy baby. She was happy, slept a lot, and gave us no trouble. I did have to carry her around each night before she would drift off to sleep, because I couldn't bear to hear her cry when I put her in the crib. But she was a sweetheart, and I was a proud father. Unfortunately, my marriage to Alice was anything but sweet. Instead, it was one storm after another. To deal with growing estrangement from each other, we decided—or I should say, she demanded—that I should undergo psychotherapy. I was reluctant, but besides Marxism, our other chosen -*ism* was Freudianism, which we thought could do for the individual psyche what Marx could do for society. I began by going to a free therapy group at the student clinic, but found that I could not relate to the young interns who conducted the sessions. Some of our friends in the Madison Left told me about a therapist they were seeing in Chicago, a bus trip of a couple of hours. The shrink's name was Dr. Alan Robertson, and one of our associates simply raved about him. He gave us what amounted to a package deal: if several of us could book his services for every Saturday, we would all go in, take turns seeing him, and go back to Madison together. And so each Saturday, my wife and I along with four friends would go by car or bus to Chicago, where we walked around the lake, went to the library, or shopped until it was time for our slot.

Dr. Robertson was, to be candid, rather bizarre. He looked like a football player, very unshrinklike. But what was really strange was his announcement to us that he had discovered a new form of therapy, which he dubbed "sleep therapy." He showed me a journal article he wrote explaining his approach, which was to promote a new, deeper form of communication between patient and therapist that allowed the patient to reach the deepest levels of the unconscious. That treatment was sleep. This meant that instead of talking or engaging in traditional Freudian free association, the patient would sit back and drift off to sleep, as would the therapist. The session ended when his alarm clock woke us up. Since I arrived at the session exhausted from the demands of school, child care and the long trip to Chicago, I was very receptive to this treatment. Dr. Robertson told me that my therapy was a great success—I slept more than the others in our group, and I should be proud of my accomplishment. Indeed, I always felt good and happy when I left.

Driving back to Madison, the first thing we asked each other was "How did your session go?" I was able to one-up them easily, since I could almost always answer that I had slept through the entire fifty minutes. This produced great jealousy and hostility among my friends, some of whom had not been able to sleep and had actually tried to talk about their problems. Two of the group—my old roommate Matt and his girlfriend, Judy, who had left her husband and taken custody of their daughter—became so enamored with Dr. Robertson that they moved out of Madison and took a home right next door to him! Subsequently, I learned that Matt simply disappeared one day, leaving a note saying that he had left for good and changed his name, and that they would never find him.

When I first arrived in Madison in 1955, I was a typical New York, left-wing freshman. Eight years later I was a married man and a young father, had an M.A. under my belt, and was finishing my graduate work. Aside from socializing, folk singing and going to meetings of the *Studies* board and the Socialist Club, I spent my time in seminars, at the library, completing coursework and papers, and studying for the preliminary examination, which was necessary to qualify for permission to continue on with the doctoral dissertation.

The exam was a two-day affair of answering essay questions for eight hours each day, followed by an anxious wait for the results. When I passed, my mentor, William Appleman Williams, became a different person. Until that time, he operated according to the Navy code. You were a midshipman; you addressed him as Mr. Williams, and were perfunctory and formal. When I received the notice that I had passed, I went to his office for a scheduled appointment on my dissertation topic. I walked in and began to say "Mr. Williams," when he cut me off. "Call me Bill," he said, "really." He then suggested that we go out to a café and sit and gab. Clearly, passing the prelims was much like promotion to the officer corps. No longer was I a mere grad student, but a colleague engaged in a scholarly endeavor.

Seeking a topic different from those chosen by others of his students, I decided upon a study of the ideology of American labor leaders. Most of the following year was spent in beginning research on the topic and studying manuscripts on deposit in the State Historical Society archives, housed in one of the campus buildings. The year passed at lightning speed, and come summer, Alice and I were off to New York. The student phase of my life was over, and I felt that I was about to enter the real world.

6

My 1960s in New York City

I HAD ORIGINALLY PLANNED, AFTER SUMMER IN NEW YORK, TO return to Madison and get another teaching assistantship, write my dissertation, and then apply for a job at a good college or university. Unfortunately, the tensions of our marriage took a physical toll on Alice, and she developed a serious medical problem that required her to be near her family in New York, so we began to look for a place there. With little money, our options were slim. Fortunately, a new middle-income housing development funded with federal money had been built in what was largely Spanish East Harlem. Franklin Plaza, as the development was called, had large lawns and play areas perfect for children. Among the residents were many other young graduate students and their families, as well as scores of assorted lefties glad for an opportunity to be near "the people." So for about $100 a month, we got a two-bedroom (later three-bedroom) apartment, and most important, a new "magnet" model school staffed by the best teachers provided in a new experiment by the United Federation of Teachers. It was socialism in action, although of course, we didn't see it that way at the time.

As I look back at this period, I am amazed at the opportunities I passed up because I believed they were politically incorrect. For instance, after placing an ad for a job in the pages of the *Saturday Review,* then a middlebrow "cultural" magazine with high pretensions, I received several responses. One was from the National Industrial Conference Board, a corporate policy group in New York. After an interview, they showed me what would be my office, a large suite with giant windows overlooking downtown Manhattan. They introduced me to the woman who would be my private secretary and then showed me their swimming pool, gym and other amenities. The job—covering developments in organized labor and evaluating their impact on the business climate—was mine, they told me. As I looked at the large salary and the many perks, my thought was not that I would be able to provide for my family, but that if I took the job, I would be selling out the socialist movement. I recall asking Jimmy Weinstein about the group, and he told me they were a major corporate organization, not particularly reactionary though clearly part of the apparatus of the "ruling class." I had no choice. I phoned the man who had interviewed me and turned down their generous offer.

Another job offer came from KLH, manufacturer of the high-quality stereos and speakers all my friends had. Go to a college dorm in those days and you would find a KLH portable system. The founder and president of the firm wrote to say he was impressed with my ad, and he was certain that if I was willing to give up a teaching career in the academy, I would do quite well as an executive with his firm. I knew nothing about business, high fidelity and stereo equipment; and of course, the worst thing I could do, I thought, was to work in the world of capitalism. I went to the KLH headquarters in Cambridge for an interview, and then turned down the offer.

Finally, I thought that perhaps I could work in the news media, where my left-wing perspective would bring some balance to what I believed was the otherwise biased reporting that appeared on television. I was a few decades too early. If I were looking for a job in journalism today, my left-wing activity would be an asset, but back then, I realized that my bias had to be hid. My friend Jimmy Weinstein, who was now editing *Studies on the Left* in New York City, got an interview for me at ABC television news, where one of his family's friends, a top female reporter, had arranged one of the first TV interviews with Fidel Castro. I had an interview with her producer and one of the producers for the local ABC news. They asked me what I could offer them. I recall answering that I had no knowledge of production technique, the news business, or anything else that one did in television, but that it sounded like an interesting career. They looked at me as if I were in the wrong place—which I certainly was, and I left this time without any job offer.

In the end, I decided to do what scores of others in Ph.D. limbo seemed to do in those years while waiting for something better to turn up: I took a job as welfare investigator with the New York City Department of Welfare. Here, at least, I would be able to work in behalf of the people. In those early welfare state days, the city's poor did not automatically receive welfare checks. Their situation had to be investigated thoroughly, and then investigators had to decide what monthly stipend they should receive and whether or not they were capable of handling the funds. We were told, for example, to make sure that money for food and clothing did not go toward a television set or a second telephone line.

After two weeks of training, I was ready for my first foray into the field. Assigned to central Harlem, I was to walk alone through the neighborhoods visiting families in one dingy apartment after another. As a young, white, Jewish boy, I did not look forward to traipsing through the black ghetto by myself. "Don't worry," our trainer told us, "the black book you'll carry is your key to survival. When they see it, you'll be treated deferentially, since they want you to give them money." I wasn't convinced. "Oh," our trainer added as he dismissed me, "just carry enough money for train fare and a small lunch. That way if you're mugged, you won't have anything valuable for them to take."

After two weeks, I was desperate to leave. I began to search the want ads each day. It never occurred to me to phone the corporate policy firm or KLH to ask if there was still an opening. I might not feel comfortable among the black proletariat, but I was not going to be a sellout. Finally I noticed an enticing ad for a writer-researcher job for something to be called *The American Negro Reference Book,* an encyclopedia of the Negro experience in America. This would be a safer way of dealing with the issue of race. I immediately called for an interview with the project's director, a black man named John P. Davis. I had never heard of Davis, but a little research quickly indicated that he was indeed the same John P. Davis who had been head of a major Communist front, the National Negro Congress, in the 1930s.

Since he had been a Communist, I knew he would not reject me for the job because I was a white. After all, the party's slogan had always been "black and white, unite and fight."

When I finally met Davis, he greeted me tersely: "Since you're obviously someone who can't finish his Ph.D. dissertation [which I actually had just started writing] this will be a good job for you." And so I left the Welfare Department. My last day there, I was due to pick up my final paycheck at closing time, 5 P.M. But early in the day, people began to run hysterically through the offices, heading for home. We turned on the radio and heard the announcement that President John F. Kennedy had been shot. I ran to the pay office, demanded my salary early, and left for home, where my wife and I, like the rest of the nation, were glued to the television set for much of the next few days.

John P. Davis wanted me to start immediately—the day after the assassination—on my new job, researching and writing entries for *The American Negro Reference Book*. Unfortunately, the new president, Lyndon B. Johnson, had declared an official day of mourning, and virtually all of New York City closed down. But Davis felt that his project should march forward, so he demanded that I come to the office over the weekend. Since I was specializing in labor history, he suggested that I begin with an entry on the labor movement and civil rights; I could start by consulting the AFL-CIO's official civil rights spokesman, and also obtain copies of his articles and statements. I consented, but said that I also wanted to interview the NAACP's labor expert, a white intellectual named Herbert Hill, who had made a name for himself by regularly protesting the incipient racism of the trade union movement, particularly those craft unions that had been part of the older American Federation of Labor.

I phoned Hill and scheduled an appointment with him at the NAACP's national offices, then in the original Freedom House building in New York, opposite the public library on West Forty-fourth Street. Hill was sharp, outspoken and immediately confrontational. Viewing me as an enemy, he informed me that since I was going to obtain the viewpoint of the AFL-CIO, which he condemned as a racist institution, he was going to protest and use his office to quash the entire project I was working on. He put in a call to Davis, and announced his intention to do what he could to stop the project, unless the entry on the labor movement and civil rights had only his—and the NAACP's—point of view.

By the time I got back to the project office, Davis was waiting for me. Over the next hour, he blamed me for what had happened and then immediately fired me. Because of my stupidity, he said, I had jeopardized his entire project and had become a tool of the antilabor views of Herbert Hill and the NAACP. I was without a job, and desperate. I had one recourse. I stormed back into Hill's office and told him that what he had done was reprehensible. Because I had been foolish enough to try to include his viewpoint, I had been fired from a job I badly needed. Hill thought for a minute and then responded with his own counteroffer: "I'll hire you at the same salary as Davis," he said, "to be a researcher and writer for my projects." I accepted on the spot, and went to work for Herbert Hill.

People must have wondered how Hill, a full-time organizer and activist for the NAACP, had the time to turn out the articles that appeared over the next year. The answer was that I researched and wrote them entirely on my own. Hill would look over my work and hardly make any changes whatsoever. But he made it clear from day one that he was paying me well for complete anonymity and secrecy. No one was to know I was working for him or even knew him. If I needed to obtain material and files from the NAACP office, as in fact I often did, I was to claim that I was writing a paper. I was not to talk to him or acknowledge him in any way, should I ever bump into him. He would inform me of what topics he wanted researched, and what he wanted to say. The rest was up to me.

Some of the topics Hill chose were lengthy and involved real research—not the kind of essay that could be knocked off in a few days. He desperately wanted to build up a pedigree as more than a labor organizer for the Movement. Since I was his employee, and my own role would be anonymous, I did what he wanted.

My job with Hill lasted a little over one year. Not wanting to work for him a second longer than I had to, I used my spare time to apply for teaching jobs in the New York City area. In those days, it was possible for those who had completed all coursework for the Ph.D. but hadn't finished their dissertation to get a job. When a position was announced at Kingsborough Community College in Sheepshead Bay, Brooklyn, a two-year institution of the City University of New York, I applied. The chairman of the history department was Marc Karson, a little-known academic historian who came from the ranks of the old Socialist movement and had written a labor history centering on the unions and politics. Not only did Karson warm to me, but also he asked that I research and write an article that he would sign as co-author. Probably that got me the job. Kingsborough, however, was filled with vicious academic quarrels, and the next year I moved to another new two-year institution, Queensborough Community College in Bayside, New York, where I would work— as well as at the new Graduate Center of the City University—for the next thirty years.

The workload at Queensborough was high and the salary low. To make ends meet, I took summer jobs at other City University campuses and taught nights at both the Polytechnic Institute of New York and Rutgers University in Newark, New Jersey. But eventually things improved after the faculty of the City University campuses unionized and became affiliated with the powerful New York City teachers' union, so the subsequent contract tied our salaries to those of the city school system. Then CUNY faculty became among the highest-paid professors in the nation's university system.

I must have had a tremendous amount of energy. During the next five years, I managed to spend time with my wife and daughter, have an active social life, and become involved in campus politics and life, while also writing my dissertation and my first book. When the summer teaching session was over, we went to Alice's family's summer home in Indian Lake, New York, where I locked myself in a room every day with my portable typewriter.

I regarded the other graduate students I had studied with in Madison as careerists. I saw the Movement, not the academy, as the center of intellectual life. It all seemed to be happening in New York. The city was torn apart at the seams when a local group of black nationalists in Ocean Hill–Brownsville, the all-black section of Brooklyn, instituted a program of "community control" in which local school boards, funded by the Ford Foundation, assumed the task of hiring and firing school employees. Acting precipitously and with obvious malice, they moved first by dismissing white Jewish teachers, despite their years of solid teaching, seniority, and no bad reports about their job performance. The new head of the United Federation of Teachers, Albert Shanker, moved immediately to strike the entire school system until the New York City Board of Education rescinded the illegal action. Although my daughter, ironically, was attending a magnet school led by the UFT, my wife and I joined with local black militants and white radicals to keep the school open, despite the picket lines and despite the blatant antilabor bias of the Ocean Hill–Brownsville militants.

It was the antiwar movement, though, that galvanized us and gave our lives meaning. I joined a citywide group called the Committee to Stop the War in Vietnam, which on a national basis aligned itself with those who wanted unilateral withdrawal from Vietnam rather than negotiations. Our intention was never so much to end the war as to use antiwar sentiment to create a new revolutionary socialist movement at home. Maximalism was the order of the day. When Norman Thomas died in 1967, I wrote what may have been the only published negative assessment of his life. Most obituaries heralded Thomas as the nation's conscience, a man of principle who had turned out to be right about a great deal. Of course, Thomas was against the war in Vietnam; he had made a famous speech in which he said he came not to burn the American flag but to cleanse it. But for radicals like myself, that proved he was a sellout. His opposition to the war was so tame, I argued, that he actually helped the American ruling class. I claimed that Thomas's opposition to LBJ's bombing campaign was only a "tactical" difference with the president. Thomas's chief sin, in my view, was to have written that he did not "regard Vietcong terrorism as virtuous." He was guilty of attacking the heroic Vietnamese people, instead of the United

States, which was the real enemy of the world's people. My final judgment was that Thomas had "accepted the Cold War, its ideology and ethics and had decided to enlist in fighting its battles" on the wrong—the anti-Communist—side.

Students for a Democratic Society had created an academic affiliate for professors, and I joined the New York City branch. Our group put all its effort into demanding "immediate withdrawal" from Vietnam and combating the moderate slogan of "Negotiations Now" favored by social democrats, liberals, and, ironically, the American Communist Party. Instead of really paying attention to the war, most of our time was spent in internal dispute with the Trotskyist Socialist Workers Party, which through shrewd Leninist manipulation had taken over the national umbrella antiwar group, the Mobilization to End the War, or the Mobe, as it was generally called. The Trotskyists already had their own Leninist cadre organization, and they intended to make the Mobe a recruiting ground for their self-proclaimed vanguard party.

Hence the Trotskyists tried to get the best-known establishment and liberal names to participate in their rallies, while political points would be left to the SWP and its paper, *The Militant*. We, on the other hand, sought ideological agreement on a socialist strategy geared to organizing what we called the "new working class." The result was a series of endless, stormy meetings. I can recall numerous times when Stanley Aronowitz, then a union organizer and now a professor at the City University and its most renowned Marxist intellectual, would call me near midnight and say that I had to come to another emergency meeting. Once, we began a regular session 8 P.M. and were still going at 3 A.M. That, after all, was the method by which the Trotskyists always won: by outlasting the opposition.

Our ideology was expressed in what became an influential theoretical statement written by a young man named David Gilbert, who while in SDS had developed the theory of a "new working class" growing from the student community. Later, Gilbert would emerge as one of the major leaders of the most radical branch of SDS, the so-called Weathermen faction, whose name was taken from a line of Bob Dylan's ("you don't need a weatherman to know which way the wind blows"). As the group turned to advocating violence and planting bombs, and its members went into hiding, they became known as the "Weather Underground," with the slogan "John Brown—live like him." After the Weather Underground had more or less disbanded at the end of the 1970s, Gilbert became involved in the notorious Brinks robbery in Nyack, New York, during which police and bank guards were killed. Gilbert would be sentenced to life in prison for his role in that action. He may have lived like John Brown, but fortunately for him, the state did not seek to inflict on him the fate suffered by his hero in the Civil War years.

A decade before the Brinks job, however, Gilbert had become the leading spokesman in SDS for ideological opposition to the Maoists of the Progressive Labor Party (the PL), who had sought to infiltrate the organization at Columbia University and to take it over nationwide. The PL favored a traditional Leninist working-class-oriented strategy, seeking what they called a student-worker alliance in which students would join the ranks of the only revolutionary class that existed, the blue-collar factory workers. Gilbert and his New Left comrades argued more realistically that in fact students were the "workers" of the new economy, and had in effect been proletarianized by their own condition. One of our bibles was a West Coast essay that had been reprinted everywhere, called "The Student as Nigger," which made that same argument more crudely. Gilbert came regularly to the meetings of our local "Independent Committee to End the War in Vietnam," which was our official Mobe affiliate group. Working to end the war and organize students, he argued, was our true work as revolutionaries.

On the surface, it seemed unlikely that small Queensborough Community College, of suburban Bayside, Queens (near the border of New York City and Long Island), would be affected by the turmoil of the Sixties. But the right mix was there: highly intelligent middle class, largely white students, the Vietnam draft, and a small corps of dedicated radical faculty members and students, who of course had formed their own campus SDS chapter. The president of the college, Kurt Schmeller, was still in his twenties, the youngest college president in the country. A graduate of Princeton with a Ph.D. in European history, Schmeller had been chosen by a faculty committee at Queensborough because its members assumed that his youth would help to create a vibrant campus at the new college.

Watching the famed National Teach-in staged in Washington, D.C., I quickly decided that the time was ripe to organize a local counterpart at Queensbourgh. The headliner at our teach-in would be my friend Sol Stern, who, after leaving the University of Iowa, moved to Berkeley and became one of three main editors of the New Left popular magazine *Ramparts*. Stern had recently returned from Communist Czechoslovakia, where he traveled to meet with representatives of the Vietcong. Always a first-class debater, he wowed the students from the beginning of his speech, "Some Americans fight the Vietcong in their own country; others of us go to meet and talk with them in Czechoslovakia." We also brought George McGovern, at that time a relatively unknown South Dakota senator, to present one of the first major speeches he gave against the war.

The events on campus, however, quickly escalated from speeches to sit-ins in the administration offices and the demand for cancellation of all classes. By a strange twist of fate, future Brinks terrorist Gilbert and his girlfriend Laura Foner, daughter of the Communist historian Philip S. Foner and later a member of the Weather Underground, had been assigned by SDS to the Queensborough campus. Among other revolutionary actions, they spray-painted the library building with the slogan "Avenge the Death of Fred Hampton," referring to the shootout in Chicago during which local police stormed the Black Panther's home and killed him in the ensuing confusion. Now, many decades later, the slogan still sits on the brick walls of the building, all efforts to remove it having failed. I doubt if anyone looking at it today even knows what it means.

But the high point of the Queensborough disturbances, in which Foner and Gilbert served as field marshals, was triggered by a local issue: the failure of the English department to grant tenure to a professor named Don Silberman, who at the time happened to be a member of the Maoist Progressive Labor Party, although when his tenure was denied, no one on the campus—certainly not his colleagues—had any inkling of this. Once his academic qualifications failed him, Silberman suddenly went public as a Communist, surprising us all by claiming that he had been denied tenure for political reasons. He argued that despite the unanimous recommendation of his department that he be permanently hired, a judgment seconded by the college's Promotion and Budget Committee, he had been fired because of his political views.

Silberman knew that liberal guilt would allow him to resurrect the ghost of Joe McCarthy as an ally in his cause. He even convinced the cartoonist David Levine, whose work appeared regularly in the *New York Review of Books,* to draw a caricature of QCC's president, Kurt Schmeller, flying on a broomstick and carrying Silberman off to his fate. Levine accepted Silberman's premise, drawing Schmeller to resemble Joe McCarthy. This cartoon was copied and handed out in leaflets and reprinted in the pages of the Progressive Labor Party's regular publications.

Having defined himself as a victim of political persecution, Silberman and a couple of other academics, both of them professional radicals also denied tenure, immediately went to work organizing a campus sit-in. They managed to convince prominent personalities who knew nothing of the real issues to appear and speak at the first rally, including the novelist Joseph Heller, then at the peak of his *Catch-22* fame, and even President John F. Kennedy's former chief counsel, Ted Sorenson. As the SDS leaders explained in their meetings with the students, the strike was not just in defense of the three dismissed professors, but also against the "system."

Emulating their fellow students at the Ivy League, four hundred Queensborough students, as a front-page *New York Times* story put it, "after overpowering security guards at the door, occupied the fourth floor of the administration building." The administration warned them that unless they left, they would face arrest. The students temporarily adjourned, and soon after, twenty-five others returned to resume the occupation, "vowing to continue it until they were either arrested or their demands

were met." The administration then suspended them and called
in the police to clear the occupied area.

Two days later, faculty met and asked that the three dismissed
professors be immediately reinstated; that police not be called
unless there was a danger to life and property; and that court
orders and student suspensions be lifted. The administration
responded with a compromise offer. It agreed to reinstate the
three in the fall semester, reprimanding them with a one-
semester suspension. This offer was rejected, since the defense
committee argued that it meant they would have "no income
and a break in their service for tenure."

I offered support in a letter published in the *New York Times*,
where I repeated the false charge that Don Silberman had been
victimized because of his "private political views." I claimed that
a peaceful sit-in had resulted in five hundred members of the
Tactical Police Force appearing on campus. What I left out was
my full knowledge that the three dismissed faculty were fervent
political radicals, steeped in both the counterculture and Mao-
ism, and that what they sought above all was a politicization of
the campus. Accusing the college administration of seeking to
"preserve its authority on the basis of pure coercive power," I
charged that a virtual "reign of terror" was taking place at
Queensborough.

As it turned out, arrangements were made for the arrested
Queensborough students to serve their short jail terms during
summer session. But any hope that the campus would return
to calm was destroyed by the furious nationwide reaction to the
National Guard's April 30, 1970, killing of four Kent State students protesting the U.S. invasion of Cambodia. At Queensborough, students in the local SDS chapter, meeting sympathetic
faculty members including myself, joined in the demand for a
nationwide student strike and for the closing down of our campus. (New York City's liberal Republican mayor, John V. Lindsay,
made things much easier when he set aside a formal day of
protest in New York in memorial to the slain Kent State students.) We pledged to run voluntary "freedom schools" to
replace the enforced bourgeois education the students were getting in their regular classes.

At a rally protesting the shootings at Kent State and calling for a student strike at Queensborough, four students wearing Kent State jackets and sweaters and red armbands raised clenched fists as they strode onto the stage. Whether or not they were actually from Kent State, I could tell by their politics that they were members of the Socialist Workers Party, which also had a strong foothold in the antiwar movement. Their appearance inflamed the crowd. The dean of admissions, George Alterman, trying to prevent another sit-in or worse, came to the podium and expressed sympathy for the students' anguish, but pleaded with them not to let their feelings of the moment interfere with the business of education.

I immediately approached the microphone. The dean attempted to prevent me from speaking, and I pushed him back so hard that he almost fell to the ground. I then gave a speech that worked the assembled students into a frenzy. I repeated aloud the words of a Jefferson Airplane song, "Volunteers," in which they urged their listeners, "Got to Revolution, Got to Revolution," and said that "one generation got old" while "this generation got no destination to hold." Echoing the Airplane, I shouted, "Pick up the Cry: Got to Revolution!" The students went wild. Before I knew it, the crowd was yelling "STRIKE! STRIKE! STRIKE!" Suddenly, a few students bolted from the audience, rushed the stage, and carried me off on their shoulders. One student ran to the flagpole and, hoisted on the shoulders of another, ripped down the American flag.

As at other campuses across the nation, our semester ended a month early. The most activist students in my class, those to whom I was the closest, had skipped previous exams and had not done their term papers, yet none of them would get failing grades. A philosophy teacher named Katherine Stabile argued that it was cheating the students to let them graduate or be advanced to the following year without having done any work. She said she intended to keep her classes going, give final exams, and not cave in to left-wing tyrants who claimed to have all virtue on their side. I, of course, had a sharp and nasty answer, which I gave in the best New Left fashion. "Some kill students with National Guard bullets while others do it with grades." It was the worst of analogies, but my side carried the argument, and no grades were required that year at Queensborough. Still, the school never sanctioned a strike, as others did.

In his recent book *The Long March,* cultural critic Roger Kimball reflects on how readily the nation's college administrators capitulated to the rising chorus of demands emanating from student radicals in the 1960s, especially at elite schools such as Cornell and Yale. Rather than stand firm on behalf of academic standards and defend the university's role as a disinterested institution of research and learning, they preferred the easier course of surrendering to the pressures of those who sought above all the politicization of the universities. Perhaps because Queensborough was the exact opposite of a Columbia, a Princeton, a Cornell or a Harvard, it was easier for the school's president and administration to defy the trend at colleges nationwide and show some backbone in the face of student and faculty protest.

My activism was not without cost. The school administration held my antics against me for years. Despite a sustained scholarly output, they regularly denied my requests for promotion to a higher rank. I filed a protest with the Academic Freedom Committee of the American Historical Association, which appointed a very distinguished group of senior professors, some from Columbia University, to investigate my case and prepare a report which argued that my case was strong—that my academic achievement would have been rewarded with promotion at any other institution.

Next, I turned to the AFL-CIO and the American Federation of Teachers affiliate on my campus to take up my case—even though my first major published work, *American Labor and United States Foreign Policy,* was devoted to the argument that organized labor was a conservative force that had as its main role the pacification of workers and their integration into the corporate state. The union representative who took up my case, my colleague Sheila Polishook—whose husband, Irwin, would eventually became the union's leader—was a fervent supporter of the war in Vietnam, a traditional Cold War liberal with whom I had regularly debated at campus events. Nonetheless, the union chapter instituted formal legal proceedings to secure my promotion, and even threatened to take my case to federal court. I was finally promoted, although the outcome did not make me rethink my ideas about the union movement.

Academic protest was something I did with my left hand. Off campus, I continued my efforts to build a new socialist movement, inspired by my old friend James Weinstein, who had brought *Studies on the Left* from Madison to New York, and needed a new venture to keep him busy once the journal had folded. Among other things, Jimmy would try running for Congress in the liberal Upper West Side of New York, on the third-party line of the Committee for Independent Political Action, or CIPA. Weinstein believed—indeed, it was the obsessive concern of his scholarly work—that the time was ripe for an avowed socialist party in America. He and Marty Sklar had been arguing on behalf of such a course for years, in the pages of *Studies* and elsewhere, including the newly formed Socialist Scholars Conference. But in the long run, Jim would find that it was far easier to found a journal than a movement. In a short time, he would move to San Francisco, where for years he presided over a magazine he named *Socialist Revolution,* which after the apparent collapse of the revolutionary project became the more mundane and reasonable *Socialist Review.* Like other radical journals, die-hard members of its West Coast collective still issue the journal long after its total irrelevance has been clear to almost everyone.

Weinstein's most successful venture was *In These Times,* a formerly weekly socialist newspaper that is now a biweekly left-wing magazine. From its ranks emerged journalists such as John B. Judis, now a senior editor of the *New Republic,* and the notorious Sidney Blumenthal, *éminence noir* of the Clinton administration. But that was all in the future of Weinstein's socialist odyssey. While he was still in New York City, he did what he could to form an elite group that would create a new socialist party. For one year, we met almost every week. What our group lacked in representation from the working class, it made up in left-wing historians, including such luminaries as the late Christopher Lasch, who often came in from Rochester to attend our sessions; the late Warren Sussman, the cultural historian from Rutgers University who was an old Wisconsin friend of Weinstein's; and Eugene D. Genovese, who would become the nation's most prominent historian of slavery in America. For weeks we dickered over what statement we should issue to propel the movement into public view, and what role students would have vis-à-vis the distinguished academic professionals. Genovese was always concerned that any new social movement respect rank and hierarchy. "I'll be in the same movement with student comrades," he said, "but they'd better realize that they are talking to Professor Genovese, and that if we publish a journal, those of us with rank must be listed separately." He didn't have to worry. The organization never really got going and never produced a new journal. Undoubtedly, Gene's frustration at our inability to move is what led him to put his formidable energy into creating his own journal, *Marxist Perspectives,* in 1978.

We did, however, manage to create the intellectual group we named the Socialist Scholars Conference. The purpose of the organization was to create an atmosphere in which socialist scholarship would be taken seriously, and in which Marxists in the academy could show that they were producing work of merit that had a role to play in the intellectual marketplace. The first conference was held at Columbia University. The keynote speaker, Conor Cruise O'Brien, was mugged on his way to the event by neighborhood black thugs, who failed to differentiate him from the regular white racist "honkies."

The second Socialist Scholars Conference was held at the old Commodore Hotel, now the site of the Grand Hyatt on East Forty-second Street in New York; the rundown old-line hotel suited a socialist meeting. The highlight was a panel on the meaning of "Socialist Man" featuring Isaac Deutscher, the esteemed, Polish-born, British biographer of Lenin, Stalin and Trotsky. For Communists, Deutscher was anathema, since he was a fierce critic of what he considered Stalin's betrayal of Lenin's revolution. But for Trotskyists, he was a bridge to the Soviet state, since he praised Stalin for maintaining the essence of the revolutionary state and bringing it to the point where it could meta-

morphose into something decent. For those of us who saw ourselves as critics of the old pro-Soviet Left, and who still defended
the Communist idea, Deutscher arrived as a godsend—the intellectual hero we had been searching for. We met him at New
York's international airport, where he emerged from the plane,
pipe in hand, filling its bowl with ... South African tobacco! One
of our group, Helen Kramer, a former *Studies* editor, screamed,
"Mr. Deutscher, how can you be smoking South African
tobacco?" Our revolutionary hero, it turned out, might have
known everything about Russia in 1917, but he knew nothing of
apartheid in 1970. Blushing, he awkwardly walked to an ashcan
and threw his entire can of tobacco away.

Deutscher appeared on a panel along with one of our fellow
radical academics, an economics professor named Shane Mage.
He was an orthodox Trotskyist, a founder of the ultrasectarian
and pure Spartacist League, a sect that had split off from the
Trotskyist Socialist Workers Party because of some now forgotten doctrinal difference. (Mage proudly told everyone, "the SWP
bounced me for Menshevism.") But unbeknown to us, by the
time we invited him to speak, Mage had gone through yet
another transformation, this one far more substantial than moving from Trotskyism to Menshevism. He had evidently met Tim-
othy Leary, the prophet of LSD, and had fallen under Leary's
hypnotic spell. Mage's speech caught us off guard, and caused
the bewildered Deutscher to cover his face with his hands. Leary,
Mage announced, was the Lenin of the new era, and his message
to "Turn on, tune in and drop out" was a call to a revolution as
profound as the one that had shaken the world in 1917.
Deutscher went white and shrieked in his unmistakable Polish
accent, "Drooogs!" The Mage manifesto, which we quickly
dubbed Acid Leninism, was unique in the annals of the Socialist Scholars. Not surprisingly, it did not find its way into the published conference papers, brought out with much fanfare by
Oxford University Press.

It was the third of our meetings that showed we had arrived.
The now well-attended conference shifted to the New York
Hilton on Sixth Avenue, with speakers including a Who's Who
in the academic Left. A packed session heard Herbert Marcuse

expound on "Radicals and Hippies: Youth Responses to the Industrial Society." The presentation was considered phony by one of the audience, a relatively unknown young man who said he was a Yippie and despised academics, socialist or otherwise. It was Abbie Hoffman, who appeared in a cowboy suit with two toy guns, shooting caps as he rushed onstage. Lighting up a joint, Hoffman demanded that Marcuse stop talking and start smoking. Marcuse, who postured as an advocate of the counterculture, looked on aghast as Hoffman continued to rant and rave, causing the session to end in pandemonium—which was no doubt his purpose.

The intellectual-political activity of the Socialist Scholars reached its culmination at the annual conference of the American Historical Association in 1969. The "Radical Caucus," to which I belonged, introduced a resolution at the AHA business meeting calling for U.S. withdrawal from Vietnam. Our leaders were Staughton Lynd, a Yale history professor who would take a famous propaganda journey to Vietnam with Tom Hayden, and eventually be dismissed from his job and move on to become a labor lawyer; and Arthur Waskow, then a New Left leader and later an Orthodox Jewish rabbi who became known for writing a "Freedom Seder" to be said at Passover service. We hoped that Gene Genovese, as the nation's most distinguished Marxist historian, would join in our efforts and even choose to lead the fight.

Genovese, as everyone knew, was himself in the thick of the fight over Vietnam taking place at Rutgers University, where he was a professor. He had given a speech back in 1965 at one of the first teach-ins, in which he had condemned the war as an American "war of aggression." He went on to add, in carefully chosen words that would nevertheless come back to haunt him, "unlike most of my distinguished colleagues ... I do not fear or regret the impending victory of the Vietcong. I welcome it." When Gene uttered these words, it produced an immediate maelstrom. Richard M. Nixon publicly called on Rutgers to fire Genovese, but the governor of New Jersey, a Democrat, defended the professor's right to make such a speech on classic First Amendment grounds.

Since Gene was a self-professed revolutionary, who even had for a short while been a member of the Maoist Progressive Labor Party, we expected that he would be a strong supporter of the resolution we had put before the AHA membership. So we were shocked when we learned that Gene would lead the forces opposed to our resolution! He pointed out that passing such a resolution would in effect bind historians to advocate a position they may not necessarily believe, and to teach that position even if they strenuously disagreed with it. Should it pass, he argued in a moving and powerful address, it would serve only to further politicize the profession. Nonpolitical historians who rejected the motion would then have no choice but to resign. His closing remarks were meant to provoke, and we greeted them with boos. The New Left supporters of the withdrawal resolution, he said, were "totalitarians," and he called upon the majority of the members to isolate them and "put them down hard, once and for all." Conservative members of the AHA cheered, as we radicals stood there speechless.

7

The Personal is Political

As I struggled to earn a living and raise a family, I found that my marriage was beginning to unravel. When I took the job at Queensborough, Alice enrolled in the M.A. program at Queens College, the flagship school of the City University of New York. Work, Movement activity and friends gave us a full life and a busy schedule. Then, our son Daniel was born on March 23, 1969. What should have been a time for great joy and happiness was instead the beginning of our slide away from each other. Alice began to see a psychologist, a man who at times met with his patients for drug sessions where they got stoned on grass and LSD, which he had convinced them was part of an advanced therapeutic technique. He encouraged her to think of leaving me. The sessions ended when her analyst died of a heart attack in the middle of an acid session with one of his other patients.

We probably would have stuck it out if left to our own devices, but the Movement was turning toward the politics of personal relationships. The radical feminism of the early women's liberation movement, the call to "smash monogamy," and the scorn heaped on sound relationships as examples of "bourgeois possessiveness" were destabilizing relationships far stronger than ours.

Alice had joined one of the early consciousness-raising groups, and the women she met there encouraged her to break up our family in the interests of her own "liberation." She embarked on a series of affairs and flirtations, which according to Movement standards I was supposed to tolerate, but which actually were deeply painful and humiliating. Finally she became involved with one particular man, carrying out her affair in deep secrecy. It was always easy for her to find an excuse to be off with her new lover while offering me a plausible alibi for her absence, such as the need to spend the evening in the medical library at Mt. Sinai Hospital, the only place she could find the resources for her M.A. work in physiological psychology.

It turned out that the man she was having the affair with was a friend of mine named David Gelber, who was then serving as the editor of Dave Dellinger's magazine, *Liberation*. Gelber was in fact one of the most prominent Movement personalities: the staff director for the famed Mayday 1971 protest in Washington, D.C., where demonstrators were arrested en masse throughout the city, as well as the man who ran one of the largest Washington demonstrations against the war, put on by the Mobe.

When the Movement marches withered during the Nixon years, Gelber would become the news director of the flagship New York Pacifica station, WBAI. He went from Pacifica to the local NBC news station in New York, first as an on-air news reporter, and soon as a producer. Within a few years, he would become a top-level CBS news producer, working with Dan Rather on the evening news, then with *60 Minutes,* later with Peter Jennings on ABC, then finally settling in as a senior producer for Ed Bradley on *60 Minutes.*

I did not suspect Gelber's involvement with my wife, since we had friendly contact at *Liberation* and he frequently came to dinner at our apartment; the seeming depth of his friendship, in fact, helped to cover up the affair. During the Christmas break, he even traveled to Hawaii with Alice on a Movement junket that Dellinger was sponsoring. Again, my wife had an apparently reasonable excuse for being gone. Her sister lived in California, and since she was having trouble in her marriage, Alice said that she needed to be there with her. She phoned regularly from Hawaii, telling me that she was at her sister's. Once, I called there. Her sister said she was out, and then quickly phoned Alice in Hawaii, who called me back a little while later.

Finally, Alice and David decided they wanted to live together. I remember the shock and hurt I felt when she informed me coldly that she was in love with Gelber, and intended to move in with him and begin a new life—one that would also be "very good for the kids," since they both liked him a lot. "Everyone gets divorced nowadays," she said matter-of-factly. "It doesn't hurt children at all." She said she would be staying at friends' homes until she and Gelber could get their own place.

I waged a desperate fight to save the marriage. Instead of an immediate breakup, what followed were a few months of tortured ambiguity, in which Alice would move out to a friend's home for a day or so, and then return, saying she had decided to stay married after all. When summer came, we had bought an inexpensive trailer which was put up on the property of a Movement facility in upstate New York, part of an old pacifist community she had heard about from Dave Dellinger. She stayed up there with our children, while I taught summer session and came up for long weekends. Sometimes, she would call and tell me not to come, because she had decided to have Gelber come instead and wanted time to decide whether to choose him or me. Finally, she called to tell me that she wanted the marriage to last, and that I should come up for the duration of the summer, and that she had told Gelber it was over. I felt relieved. But after I arrived, she suffered a severe burn when the oven exploded, an accident she blamed on my presence. It was an omen, she said, that showed her she had made the wrong decision. When we returned to the city, Alice joined Gelber and a group of Movement activists in a brownstone shared between three or four families, which they had dubbed "The Commune." They had their own bedroom, and shared a common living room, kitchen and dining room.

I took a long-awaited sabbatical to try to dig out of the wreckage of my life. I spent most days severely depressed, sleeping all night and half the day, and then shut up alone watching television until I crawled into bed. Gradually, I forced myself to start going out. One of the places I discovered in the Chelsea district of downtown Manhattan was called, appropriately, "The Wild Mushroom," a name that evoked the druggie pleasures of psilocybin and other psychedelics. The Mushroom was a place inhabited by the hip and radical of the city, who moved there to escape what once was "authentic" in the Village, but which by now had become tourist traps for out-of-staters and suburban residents seeking the Village experience. Among those who inhabited the place were the black radical poet, writer and singer Julius Lester; the counterculture guru Paul Goodman; and my good friend Danny Kalb, a blues singer and founder of the Blues Project, a seminal New York Sixties-era blues/rock group. I started making friends and finding a social network, and eventually even began to date again.

I had Daniel and Laura every other full weekend, and every Sunday. Holidays and summers, they divided their time between us. My lawyer wanted me to go to the wall in suing for custody, since he thought I could prove that Alice had not been a good mother. But I didn't have the stomach for such a sordid fight, so I rejected his advice.

After several months, I had picked up an active social life—very active, in fact. Making up for what I now regarded as lost time with Alice, I hitched up with virtually any woman I was attracted to who crossed my path. It was a good time to be single: everyone available, and almost no one thought twice about immediately hopping into bed on the first date. I had never thought myself particularly attractive to women, but suddenly I had a full dance card and even got a reputation as a womanizer. Some of the things I did were questionable, but in the period when smashing monogamy was the new standard of the Movement, I could always rationalize my behavior as helping to free society from bourgeois definitions of reality.

At the Wild Mushroom, an acquaintance of mine fixed me up with a friend of his. Her name was Judy, and she was an extremely pretty, outgoing and freewheeling woman, who believed in free sex anytime and anywhere. She was raising a young son and had no job, but considered herself an artist and a filmmaker, and in fact at times managed to find work in theater and film in exchange for sexual favors. I was to learn, after getting more and more involved with her, that she also was a serious alcoholic, who after some days of sobriety would end up dead drunk, crazed and violent.

Having started research on a new book, I asked Judy to accompany me cross-country to Washington State where I had to do work in a West Coast archive. We headed out in our own version of *On the Road,* in which Judy would sometimes drink herself into a stupor, and at other times insist on rounds of non-stop sex. Somewhat of an exhibitionist, she insisted that we have sex on top of Mount Rushmore, where she hoped that perhaps other tourists would come upon us and see what we were doing. I now don't understand why or even how I did such things. Probably it was the cumulative effect of too much marijuana.

After I finished my work at a university library in Washington, we drove down the coast to San Francisco. As we drove into the city, we heard news on the radio about the shooting death of Jonathan Jackson, brother of the imprisoned black revolutionary George Jackson. The younger Jackson had brought smuggled firearms into the courthouse in Marin County during a hearing on his brother's case. He took the judge hostage, and in the melee that ensued when he tried to get away, both he and the judge were killed.

Judy and I stayed at James Weinstein's lovely house in the hills of San Francisco, and spent the days and nights visiting friends and making contacts. The most memorable excursion took place in Berkeley, where some former students of mine from Queensborough arranged a lavish dinner in my honor. They asked if they should invite their friend Bob Scheer. I said absolutely. Scheer, who with Warren Hinckle had been one of the original editors of *Ramparts* during the magazine's most notorious period, had temporarily retreated from public life, and was working at a children's nursery and living full-time in the most radical of all the radical Berkeley communes, the so-called "Red Family." The commune had been practicing with firearms in the Berkeley hills, but most of its attention was directed to sexual politics and to questions such as whether or not it was "bourgeois" to want to close the bathroom door while using the toilet. A few weeks before I got to California, the Red Family's most famous member and Scheer's bitter rival, Tom Hayden, had been expelled for the sin of sexism.

The dinner party went well. Scheer was incredulous at the affection my former students had for me. "I've never seen anything like this," he said. "How come these kids are so enamored with you?" He seemed perturbed that he was not the center of attention. Perhaps to get even, he flirted with Judy throughout the meal. At evening's end, Scheer asked us to spend the next day or so with him at the Red Family. "You've got to come and see what we're up to," he said. "You need to see what we've created."

So the next day, Judy and I showed up early in the morning at the Red Family. The place seemed to be in chaos. One woman was in the midst of childbirth, ready at any moment to deliver in the living room. Men, women and kids were standing around, encouraging her between her groans. "Isn't it great," Scheer said. Then he took us away from the den of childbirth on a tour of the house, introducing us to various people, before we sat down to talk politics. "I've given up the fast lane," Scheer said. "People don't believe it. They ask me, where are you working? What publication are you with? They don't realize that I've never had the kind of satisfaction I now have, working with kids in the nursery and living with the Red Family." His appointed job was as head teacher of the collective's school, called Blue Fairyland. As he described his daily routine, he sounded like someone trying hard to convince himself that life was great, and not doing a good job of it.

At the time, my friend Louis Menashe and I had a regular radio program on the Pacifica Network, a weekly political discussion show in which we interviewed Movement figures and engaged in political and theoretical discussion. Since Scheer was still considered an important figure in the Left—despite the "discipline" he had been forced to accept by the feminists in the collective—I got out my trusty, top-of-the-line SONY that WBAI had recommended we purchase, and began the interview. Scheer, however, said that he would talk on the record about only one topic—the only one that mattered—the realization of the socialist utopia in Kim Il Sung's North Korea.

For over two hours, Scheer talked and talked about the paradise he had seen during a recent visit to North Korea, about the greatness of Kim Il Sung, about the correct nature of his so-called *juche* ideology—evidently a word embodying Kim's redefinition of Marxism-Leninism in building communism against all obstacles and with the entire world in opposition. Others in the Movement had, of course, found heaven on earth in places like Cuba and even China (Nicaragua and Grenada were yet to come). Scheer had one-upped them all by discovering paradise in Pyongyang. Scheer's interest in North Korea was the result of its offer of sanctuary to his protégé, Black Panther Eldridge Cleaver, who fled there to escape prosecution. While there, Cleaver released a half-hour documentary film in which he talked on camera to Scheer and extolled both the virtues of his new communist paradise (which he would leave as soon as possible) and the end of the Huey Newton faction of the Black Panther Party, which had declared war on Cleaver and his followers.

Our interview went on and on, and Scheer absolutely refused to discuss any other topic except for Kim and North Korean communism. At one point I asked him incredulously, "Bob, do you really believe this crap?" Scheer responded with complete earnestness that he did—that Kim had charted out a path that other nations could and should take as an example of the art of the possible. When I returned to New York and played the tape for the producers at Pacifica-WBAI, it was too far out even for them, and they refused to air it.

After the interminable interview ended, leaving me recalling Woody Allen's famous words to Annie Hall's demented brother, "I have to go now, I'm due back on planet earth," Scheer suggested that we take a drive through the Berkeley hills. Saying goodbye to his estranged wife—a tall, good-looking blonde named Ann Weils, whom Scheer had used for a pose in a famous *Ramparts* cover on feminism and who had two-timed him with Tom Hayden during a radical junket to Hanoi—Scheer told us that this was the day for the Family's meeting of the women's liberation consciousness-raising group, and that men in the commune had to absent themselves.

Scheer, Judy and I got into my car, and off we went. We were all sitting in the front seat. Before I knew it, Scheer had his hand around Judy's shoulder and began to fondle her breasts, and at the same time, started to kiss her. Judy, of course, was so stoned that she didn't know what was happening, although she was never one to turn down a sexual overture in any case. "What the hell's going on?" I yelled at him. "This is my girl; we're traveling through the country together, and probably will live together when we get back to New York." I slammed on the breaks and pulled the car over. Jumping out and running to the passenger side of the car, I opened the door, pulled Scheer out, ran back to the driver's seat, and left him standing on the road screaming, "How will I get back? Stop the car!" That was the last time I laid eyes on Bob Scheer.

Back in New York, I made the mistake of moving into a Brooklyn brownstone with Judy, an arrangement that lasted a month or so. During that time, Judy insisted I try psychedelics. I resisted. But then, when she kept insisting, I agreed to try a little pill she "thought" was psilocybin but might very well have been LSD. Naturally, it turned out to be a nightmare. For five full days, I lived in a state of virtual terror. My "trip" had the same qualities others reported: shapes and forms taking life and leaping out of the walls in front of me—monsters, snakes, devils, anything my imagination conjured up. I remember being frozen in fear, not being able to speak, walk or even move. I lay in bed for two full days, dozing off, then waking up and hallucinating, then falling asleep again, and sometimes managing to scream in sheer terror. Judy kept telling me, "It's nothing; you're just having a bad trip"—a line out of Woodstock ("don't take the brown acid") that didn't reassure. In moments of clarity, I feared that I would never recover. Finally, whatever it was that she gave me left my body, although for weeks, I had hallucinations crossing the street, driving the car, talking to someone.

Judy moved out, and I breathed a great sigh of relief. My stay in Brooklyn, however, was to be short. The main reason was that I became subject to a few major home burglaries, one obviously committed by the moving firm I had hired. Judy had recommended a friend of hers, a direct descendant of Wendell Willkie, the 1940 Republican presidential candidate, who had a small, independent moving firm that advertised in the *Village Voice*. This Willkie turned out to have been a Village dope dealer, an occupation that was evidently his main trade. The movers who arrived to do our moving job were three black men. By the time we arrived in Brooklyn, they were thoroughly stoned on grass. As they carried in the TV and stereo equipment, one of them said: "This is good stuff. It belongs to my people, who you stole it from." When I checked the inventory, a radio and turntable were already missing. A night later, before I had a chance to install new locks and a gate, the place was broken into and all my stereo equipment was gone.

I phoned Willkie, who told me, "So my men took your stuff. They deserve a nice tip." I contacted a lawyer friend, who promptly issued an injunction against the firm's bank account. We brought suit in civil court for the money I had paid them, plus the cost of the stolen property. My lawyer found out that Willkie had been convicted previously for dealing, and we presented evidence of his moving men having been under the influence of dope. The civil court judge was beside himself. "This is not a criminal or dope trial," he admonished us. In the end, I managed to retrieve whatever small amount the firm had in its bank account, which didn't come near the cost of what Willkie's men had stolen.

After I had replaced the stolen equipment, some thieves took the new bars off the windows and stole a television, my new stereo and some cameras. They came in the middle of the night, while my daughter was visiting and asleep in the living room. When I came downstairs in the morning, the windows were broken and the living room had been emptied out. I quickly found a large, three-bedroom, rent-stabilized apartment in New York's Upper West Side, took a lease on it, and moved right in. I would stay there for the next twenty years, and it still remains in my family. My son Daniel now lives there with his wife, Gina.

My major preoccupation, aside from socialism, became looking for new women. There was the neighbor from upstairs, a woman fifteen years younger who regaled me with stories of her group sex soirées. There were academics, Movement women, assorted hippie types, dancers, editors and historians. There was, as a friend of mine said, a sort of Ron in Wonderland quality to my amours. I rehabilitated the sexual self-esteem that my former wife had crushed. But I wasn't especially happy.

The Marxist revolution we had hoped for was stillborn; but the sexual revolution was alive and well. Movement women could be counted on to jump into bed immediately. Once, Barbara Garson, author of the radical play *Macbird,* a satiric look at LBJ and the Kennedy assassination, phoned to ask me to give her banjo lessons. She had got my name from Roz Baxandall, an old friend from the Madison left wing, who had told her that I would be a superb teacher. I hardly played banjo anymore, but knew enough to give a beginner some basic lessons. When I heard Barbara on the phone, I could tell from her tone of voice that she was interested in more than the banjo. I took the subway a day later to her apartment on Bank Street in the West Village. "This is a good way to get to know someone quickly," she said as we moved to the bedroom, fifteen minutes after I walked in the door. The normal roles were reversed: I wanted a relationship with Barbara, but she made it clear that what she wanted was a good time, some good sex, and someone to hang out with occasionally. I was surprised to find so many women I was falling into bed with telling me, "this doesn't mean anything"; "don't fall in love with me"; "don't get attached to me; I just want someone to go to movies with and sleep with occasionally."

At an annual convention of the Organization of American Historians in the early 1970s, I found myself sitting next to a young feminist historian named Ann B. Gordon at a showing of historian Leon Litwack's documentary film about the Sixties. "So that's why we're so fucked up," she said to me after it was over. I wasn't sure what she meant, but I knew that I felt an immediate, powerful attraction. I offered to drive her home from Boston (she was staying at her parents' home in New Haven) at the convention's end, and she accepted the offer. By the time we got to New Haven, she had agreed to come to New York with me instead. For the rest of the holiday vacation we were together, and then the semester began and Ann returned to Madison, where she was finishing her graduate work. We stayed in touch, and once I went out to visit her. But she was already involved, I found out, with another man, and anything permanent with me was clearly doomed from the start.

My odd journey through the new sexual wonderland took place as the Nixon administration was reining in American participation in the war, and the protests were beginning to dwindle. One night, in the spring of 1972, I was home watching Tom Hayden and Jane Fonda talk on PBS television about the horrors of the war, the effect of the U.S. bombing, and the need to keep up the Movement. A day or so later, an announcement was made that a group of radical academics were planning a protest at the Pupin Laboratory at Columbia University, in opposition to the lab's contract with the Department of Defense, which might be used for producing weapons to kill Vietnamese. I had not planned to go, but besides hearing the pep talk from the beautiful couple, Fonda and Hayden, I also had read Julius Lester's latest column in *Liberation,* in which he quipped that the reason so many of us went to demonstrations was that it was a good way to get laid. So I went off to the site of the sit-in carrying an extra sleeping bag, which I planned to offer to any woman I met that I might be attracted to.

At the gathering place, Alan Wolfe—now considered one of America's most distinguished sociologists and political scientists, but then, like the rest of us, a tough-minded member of the academic Left—introduced me to the woman he had just divorced, Allis Rosenberg. He wanted me to meet her because she was then teaching a course at Brooklyn College, and was preparing to start work for a history Ph.D. in the graduate program at the City University, where I was scheduled to teach a seminar. Allis was in her twenties, cute and smart, and obviously a very nice, warm and genuine person. We had actually met several years before at a party given by our mutual friend Don Bluestone. After hanging out with her a short while, I asked her the inevitable question: did she need a sleeping bag? Of course, she had not brought one of her own, and I told her she was fortunate that I had an extra one handy.

In the meantime, the directors of this last great sit-in picked some members from the leadership to break into the offices of the Columbia University physics department and rifle through the file cabinets. They found what they were looking for. Since

I was the only historian at the sit-in who was skilled in working through files and papers, they turned to me to decipher and report on the material. Emboldened by the attention that the recently published "Pentagon Papers" had received, we decided we would prepare a summary of "The Pupin Papers" and a press release, to be distributed at a press conference the following day.

We had hoped that Columbia University would repeat its tactics from the famous 1969 events, when President Grayson Kirk had called in police, and the mass arrests and ensuing violence caused a citywide uproar. This time around, however, the Columbia administration had learned its lesson: better to wait our small group out. Every hour or so, just as we were finally drifting off to sleep, we would be awakened by one of our leaders admonishing, "The police will be here any minute! Let's get ready." But the police never came. The next plan was to go away on our own terms, and release the results of our findings as the demonstrators marched out, proclaiming victory.

That required a marathon, twenty-four-hour session of document sifting, which I hosted in my new apartment. After the documents were brought over, a group of us sorted them out and I began writing a summary, which I called "Columbia's Pentagon Papers." Then I alerted the local media. Both CBS and NBC sent their reporters and cameras, but much to our chagrin, the reporter from the radical WBAI, the Pacifica station in New York City, was nowhere to be found. I took the moment to teach the media a lesson. "We're holding off the press conference until WBAI arrives," I said. "We will not speak until our own Movement representatives are here to give the whole story and the truth." The TV news team was visibly angry, and I was very pleased with myself. Of course, the Pacifica listeners already agreed with us, and the tactic made no sense. We had to phone the station, plead with them to send a reporter, and wait an hour until he arrived.

Essentially, I argued in the press release that the documents we had found revealed that Columbia's physics department—shock of all shocks—had signed contracts with the government to undertake military-related research, which we argued had been applied in Vietnam. Hence the department and the faculty were complicit in the American aggression and deserved to be exposed. We also denied breaking in to take the documents; I said that unknown sources had presented them to us.

A few years later, I wrote an article for a magazine called *Change in Higher Education,* in which I chastised intellectuals who went to work for the CIA, arguing that even if all they did was engage in analysis of data, they were still morally culpable of whatever crimes had been committed by the agency through its covert operatives. Indeed, I compared these intellectuals to academics who worked in assessment divisions of the Gestapo in Nazi Germany. The magazine called me during summer vacation, when I was renting a house in Cape Cod. The president of Columbia University, they said, had written them a letter condemning me, saying that having broken into the physics department offices in Pupin Hall, I was myself unfit to teach in any American university. In fact, I worried that the letter could have a damaging effect on my own prospects for promotion and advancement at the City University of New York, and could easily be used against me. To have the president of a major university single me out for retribution in a national academic journal was no small matter.

At that point, friends of mine on the Cape suggested that I phone Alan Dershowitz, who also vacationed in the area, for help. Dershowitz asked me whether I had indeed been arrested and convicted for breaking into Pupin Hall. I told him that no one was ever arrested, no charges of any kind had been brought, and nothing had ever happened to me. On his advice, I then wrote a registered letter to Columbia University's president, sending a copy to the magazine. I said that I considered his letter to be a malicious libel that was damaging to me personally, and that unless he withdrew it, I was prepared to sue him and the university for libel. The ploy worked. His office phoned the magazine's editor, who told me that he had asked that the letter be withdrawn and not published.

The Pupin affair turned out to be one of those nonevents the Left tried to inflate into something significant. The only thing that came of it was the beginning of a new relationship, one that would eventually lead to marriage with Allis and a lifetime of happiness. At the time, however, we began slowly. Having just come out of a short and unsatisfactory marriage, Allis was wary of entering a new relationship too quickly. Indeed, she warned me on our first date, an afternoon in Riverside Park, that it would be better if we were just good friends and didn't let things go beyond that. But I saw in Allis something different from the other women I had been involved with. She was serious and independent, and she was immune to the Movement cant that trivialized relationships. In a mature and refreshingly old-fashioned way, Allis wanted to get to know me before going further.

We had much in common. At the time, she was also a radical, having become "politicized" as an undergraduate at the University of Wisconsin during the Vietnam War. She was involved in a socialist, feminist, consciousness-raising group, and was planning to obtain a Ph.D. in history at the CUNY Graduate Center. Indeed, one of the first things she did was register for the seminar I was going to be teaching in "Labor and Radical History" at the Graduate Center, creating an awkward situation for both of us.

We had already both made separate plans for the summer before we met at the Pupin demonstrations. I had joined with other Movement friends to rent a large group house in Saugerties, New York, the upstate New York town near Woodstock, made famous by the house known as "the big pink" that was the cover of The Band's first record album. Saugerties, indeed, was the favorite site for radicals, would-be hippies, musicians and other itinerant types. Each weekend, we would drive from the city to our own hippie haven, where the thirty or more shareholders would gather, swim nude every day in the adjacent beautiful waterfall and swimming hole, get stoned, and enjoy the balmy Catskill summers. At the same time, Allis had taken a share in her own summer rental in the Berkshires near Tanglewood, Massachusetts, with several women from her New York group. So Allis and I would alternate weekends: she would come to Saugerties, and then I would drive to the Berkshires the next weekend.

In the fall, Allis began teaching in the women's studies department at Richmond College of the City University of New York. The college had become a haven for the left wing, even though it was situated in working-class Staten Island, where most of the students were Italian Catholics far removed from any sympathy or association with the faculty teaching them. At the time, the Richmond women's studies department was the only one in the entire City University, although its curriculum was soon copied throughout the system.

Allis wrote about her experiences in women's studies in a June 21, 1973, column for the *Village Voice*. She noted that students at Richmond could major or minor in the program, which hired its own staff and developed its own courses, obviously without control or supervision by the college curriculum committee. As a good feminist socialist, Allis still believed that women needed to have a separate curriculum, since they shared a "separate historical experience" from that of men. Yet she worried that these separate women's studies departments were not creating an appreciation of women's history, but might in fact be interfering with the desires of women to gain equality in the mainstream of society.

What Allis recorded in the *Voice*, and what she daily came home to tell me about, was almost unbelievable. At Richmond, she complained, certain radical women were arguing that there was one correct feminist ideology. When Allis replied that feminists could be "conservatives, liberals or socialists," her new colleagues scorned this view. In particular, gay women used an analogy with the black liberation movement, claiming to be the "most oppressed women," a position that hence "put them into the vanguard of the women's movement." They demanded that their leadership be accepted, and said that straight women had to "come to assert and recognize their own homosexuality." Allis wrote that "Radical lesbians organized to stack the program's meetings." They moved to fire faculty and administrative staff who were not gay, and defined any heterosexual women automatically as the enemy of all women. It was a display of "gay vanguardism," and its exponents soon came to classes and to the college brandishing baseball bats, which they claimed to need for protection.

We talked about what all of this meant for understanding the movement we were part of, and Allis put her finger on it. "The logic that allows straight women to meekly acquiesce to gay vanguardism," she wrote, "is similar to the process that has taken place among white radicals in their relation to the black movement." The psychological effect was to cause a "guilt trip" syndrome, with those who do not go along accused of being oppressors.

Allis's experience with radical feminism, occurring at the same time as I was beginning to harbor doubts about my ideological commitments, further brought us together. We seemed to find shrill and almost pathologically crazy behavior wherever we looked on the left. Many of our friends seemed to be going off the deep end politically. Some of them ended up in the extreme, cult-like, radical organization founded by Lyndon LaRouche, who then called himself Lynn Marcus (after Lenin and Marx) and claimed to be developing a new revolutionary working-class organization. LaRouche was full of conspiracy theories, stories of KGB-CIA plots to kidnap and brainwash him, and of secret plots to wage nuclear war, which only he and his cadre could stop.

Even the usually sober Gene Genovese gathered an academic committee of intellectuals in defense of LaRouche. When I challenged him, he responded that "we have a responsibility to come to the aid of serious working-class movements when they ask for our help." Others of our friends actually joined his group, advocating a fight against a Rockefeller-dominated world conspiracy which, in conjunction with the Queen of England, was supposedly going to take over the universe via the international drug trade. One of my friends from the faculty group, a brilliant young scientist who had traveled to Cuba and had taken part in the Chile protests with me, informed me that he had joined LaRouche, and then he began regular efforts to recruit me. Once, he phoned me late at night, sounding hysterical. "We have information that guided missiles will be falling on America tomorrow. Only concerted action by the LaRouche vanguard can stop it." He offered to give me exclusive access to the secret LaRouche war room, where he promised I would find the highest technological wizardry tied in to secret reports coming from all over the world. When I declined to get dressed and meet him, he said, "You'll regret this when you look out the window and see the missiles." Eventually, he became editor of one of LaRouche's journals, *Fusion Power,* which attempted to influence the scientific community.

In 1972, Allis and I became involved in the McGovern campaign, although she did so reluctantly (considering McGovern too right-wing). I recall attending a debate held between Herbert Marcuse and Stanley Aronowitz at the Brooklyn College law school annex, where Marcuse condemned all those opposed to voting for McGovern as people "lurking in their sectarian tents." Perhaps for that reason, Marcuse was losing his cachet with the New Left. Hearing Marcuse endorse McGovern reminded me of the last time I had heard him speak, in 1970 or 1971 at the Fillmore East, the rock and roll palace run by promoter Bill Graham, who often handed over the facility to radical groups. The hall was filled to capacity as Movement leaders including Carl Oglesby, one of the top SDS leaders, and Bernadine Dohrn, later of the Weather Underground, held their own rally and concert to carry on the struggle. The place almost erupted when Dohrn introduced Marcuse as "*Time* magazine's most favored radical," saying the words with a sneer on her face and scorn in her voice—to which Marcuse feebly responded, "I am not responsible for *Time*'s characterization of me."

Allis and I got married in October of 1975, with a simple ceremony at New York's City Hall, the place of working-class weddings. Looking at our marriage certificate years later, we noticed that the city clerk who married us was David Dinkins, future mayor of New York, who had one of his first patronage appointments at the marriage desk. It may be a cliché, but after twenty-five years of marriage, we are more in love than ever.

Allis worked hard at being a stepmother to Daniel and Laura, who came over most weekends and on many holidays, as well as a month each summer. At first it was difficult for her to adjust to the demands of helping to raise my children, but she devoted herself to the task and became happily involved in their lives. Approaching thirty, she began to long for a child of her own. After a miscarriage, she bore a daughter, named Anna after Allis's much-loved grandmother. Anna was underweight and had multiple anomalies that our doctors could not identify with any known syndrome. But she was a beautiful baby and we prayed that the prognosis was wrong. A few months after her birth, we rented a home in Cape Cod for the summer and tried to pretend that all would work out. Eventually, after a few months, it became clear that her development was abnormal. Our love for her, and her mysterious illness, drove us both into despair and depression. Unable to work, I had to take a sabbatical from school so I could spend most of my time caring for the baby and trying to get through each day. Anna died a little over a year after her birth.

Later, we had genetic counseling and were advised that since no one knew what had gone wrong, it was not likely to happen again. Soon Allis became pregnant again, and was extremely careful to avoid any undue exertion or stress that might prompt a miscarriage. Our son Michael Aaron was born in May of 1981, perfectly healthy and full of life. As I write this he is already a sophomore in college, a bright young man, a wonderful musician, and a lovely person. The joy he brought to us, so soon after our grief at Anna's death, deepened our understanding of what is truly important in life.

My parents,
Ida and Reuben Radosh,
in the 1920s.

To Mone and looks with affection and anti-fascist greetings. Irving Spain Dec 1937

LEFT: My uncle Irving Keith (né Kreichman) in his commissar's uniform; Spain, December 1937.

BELOW: My father's union at a 1930s May Day Parade in New York City.

ABOVE: I'm surrounded by my grandmother Esther Kreichman, my mother, my aunt Ann and friends; Brookwood summer colony, New York, 1938.

RIGHT: My mother's cousin Jacob Abrams and his wife, Mary, in Mexico, 1945.

Elisabeth Irwin High School
New York City

Alaska Colly 4-6-54

TOP: My Elisabeth Irwin class visits Pennsylvania coal mines, 1954.

ABOVE: Pete Seeger singing at Camp Woodland, 1950s.

LEFT: Square dancing at Camp Woodland, 1950s.

ABOVE: Playing banjo with
Marshall Brickman;
University of Wisconsin,
Madison, 1957.

BELOW: John Cohen and I
stand watching Woody
Guthrie and Ramblin' Jack
Elliott at Washington Square
Park, New York City, 1954.
*(photo by Arthur Dubinsky,
courtesy of John Cohen)*

LEFT: With Allis in Riverside Park, New York City, 1970s.

BELOW: Laura, Daniel, and Michael, summer of 1997.

ABOVE: In Jamaica with Michael Harrington and Michael Manley, 1978.

BELOW: With Ed Koch at press conference in Managua, November 1987.

ABOVE: With Nina Shea (third from left) at refugee camp in Honduras, 1986.

RIGHT: Jeff Herf, Peter Collier and David Horowitz at Second Thoughts conference in Cracow, Poland, 1989.

Socialist Lobotomies

DESPITE THE BEST EFFORTS OF THE LEFT, THE NATION'S ATTENTION was beginning to shift away from Vietnam. President Nixon had "Vietnamized" the war, withdrawing American troops to let the Vietnamese fight alone, so the draft was no longer a sword of Damocles hanging over every young man's head. We realized that the game was up. The issue that had given meaning to our lives was beginning to evaporate; and for many, this was an occasion for deep melancholy.

This would have caused more of a crisis than it did, if we hadn't still had Cuba. Living "in the belly of the beast," as we called the United States, we had regarded Castro's revolution as our great hope. As young radicals in 1959, we watched in awe as Fidel and his romantic group of *barbudos* "liberated" his small island from the grip of the American empire, which had held Cuba in its grasp since defeating Spain at the end of the nineteenth century. Fidel had done this, we insisted, as an independent radical, standing against and operating without the support of the Moscow-backed Cuban Communists. He was the first true New Left revolutionary, a man who would not compromise, a man who promised and would build a humanist revolution that would be truly democratic—not Red; not Red, White and Blue; but guerrilla green. His success loomed as the greatest feat in the history of revolution, because he had pulled off this triumph ninety miles from the greatest imperial power the world had known since Rome.

More than any other event, it was the Cuban Revolution and Fidel's victory that gave impetus and power to the youthful New Left. Fidel was only in his thirties, just a few years older than those of us in college, and we thought, if he could do it in small Cuba, there was hope for us on the imperial mainland. So as Vietnam began to fade from view, we turned our fond gaze to Cuba once again.

For years, I had wanted to visit Cuba. In Madison, shortly after Castro's victory, my commitment to my studies kept me from joining other students in the first pilgrimage of the Student Fair Play for Cuba Committee, which Saul Landau had organized. I almost got to go after my return to New York, when an old friend from the Labor Youth League, Fred Jerome, decided to organize a major student trip to Cuba.

Jerome was the son of one of the Communist Party's most feared leaders, the cultural apparatchik V. J. Jerome, whose control of the Hollywood Communists in the 1930s from his perch at party headquarters in New York City was legendary. Unfortunately, Fred inherited his father's most sectarian persona. When I saw him in New York over the holiday, I agreed to sign on. Then, Jerome gave me the conditions for working with him: I had to agree to formally join the ultraleft Progressive Labor Party, to come to their meetings on a regular basis, and to abide by the decisions made by its leadership according to the Marxist-Leninist principles of "democratic centralism." I told him that I was not ready to join PL. As we walked down the street, Fred suddenly stopped, looked at me, and said, "I cannot have anything to do with bourgeois sympathizers who are enemies of the working class."

I did attend a meeting at New York's Town Hall on West Forty-third Street off Broadway, where a large crowd came to hear a report from the youth group that had broken the embargo on travel and gone to Cuba. It was a scene of turmoil and fear. Inside, Jerome and others spoke about Castro's valiant effort to build socialism, while celebrities like actor Alan Arkin gave their support. Outside, thousands of recent Cuban refugees who now lived in Miami and New Jersey picketed and screamed. When we left the theater, if it had not been for the huge contingent of mounted police, the furious Cuban demonstrators would have savagely beaten us all. The cops guided us safely to subway entrances, lining the station in force until we could get into subway cars and flee to safety. Once again we had been saved by the fascist pigs.

Almost a decade after the Town Hall event, I finally got my chance to travel to Cuba. Sandra Levinson, who had come to New York City as a radical superstar, put the trip together. Sandy was part of the *Ramparts* editorial group associated with Bob Scheer and Warren Hinckle, and was also regarded as a hot number, known as much for her miniskirts and boots as for her radical ideology. A new group that Sandy created with Cuban help, called the Center for Cuban Studies, sponsored this trip. Its neutral-sounding name hid the reality that the center functioned as the semi-official propaganda agency for Castro in the United States. In later years, the group would help Robert Redford gain access to Cuba for his film *Havana* and would negotiate with *60 Minutes* to get them to hire Castrophile Saul Landau as a consultant and commentator, as the price for giving the program access to Cuba and an interview with Castro himself.

Our group comprised a diverse body of New York radicals— aside from myself, it included an honest but naïve left-liberal academic who taught Latin American studies at the City University; a radical psychologist who taught in the New Jersey college system; a man named Robert Cole, husband of the black Marxist Johnetta Cole, who would later become president of Spelman College and a director of the Clinton transition team for education in 1992; an activist named Suzanne Ross, a member of the Indochina Peace Campaign organized by Tom Hayden, who would found CISPES, the Committee in Solidarity with the People of El Salvador; and the highly regarded black novelist, the late Toni Cade Bambera.

As I left for Cuba, I held the sentiment voiced so eloquently by the late C. Wright Mills, the wild man of the academic New Left, whose support of the Cuban Revolution was our model. In his polemic *Listen Yankee!* Mills had written, "I am for the Cuban revolution. I do not worry about it. I worry for it and with it." Now, in the spirit of Che Guevara, who had hoped for "one, two, three many Vietnams," Cuba's propaganda agency hoped for "one, two, three many C. Wright Mills," all of whom would do precisely what the Columbia University sociology professor had done: travel to Cuba and return to spread Castro's gospel.

It was quickly apparent, though, that however serious one's intention, traveling to Cuba with Sandy Levinson inevitably made one into a revolutionary tourist, one of those starry-eyed Western intellectuals who had traveled abroad to "socialist" countries since 1917 where they saw the future, as Lincoln Steffens famously said, and saw that it worked. The classic example was given by the German New Left author Hans Magnus Enzensberger, who later wrote that while he lived in Cuba among people who were in the direst poverty, most of the "radical tourists" knew nothing of the real situation existing in paradise. "I kept meeting Communists in the hotels for foreigners," he wrote, "who had no idea that the energy and water supply in the working quarters had broken down during the afternoon, that bread was rationed, and that the population had to stand in line two hours for a slice of pizza; meanwhile the tourists in their hotel rooms were arguing about Lukacs."

And so, while the Cubans were trying to squeeze into overcrowded buses in the August heat to get to jobs where they had to work an average twelve-hour day, my comrades and I enjoyed a lobster and shrimp luncheon in the best hotel in Cuba, the Havana Libre, formally the Havana Hilton, built the year before Castro's victory. There I drank wine and chatted with Regis Debray, then the leading French supporter of Castro, who had written a book called *Revolution Within the Revolution* extolling Castro's guerrilla tactics as the single path for Third World revolt, and I sat in the sacred presence of Che Guevara's widow and other members of his family. They were engaging in the usual talk about the prospects for success of the worldwide revolution, and at the time were deeply concerned—as they were correct to have been—over the fate of Salvador Allende, their asset in Chile. After the lunch, I took the opportunity to hand Debray a mildly critical article that my friend Paul Breines had written, daring to criticize Stalinism while defending Marxism. The article had appeared in the obscure Marcusian journal *Telos,* probably read only by its own editors and a handful of other New Left intellectuals. I remember the thrill I felt: by handing the article to Debray in front of Che's family, in the heart of the center of world revolution, I saw myself as doing my part for the anti-Stalinist Left. Perhaps, I naïvely thought, even Regis Debray would see the light, and he could influence the Cuban leaders to depart from Soviet-style practices.

The next morning, we began to experience some Cuban reality. Some of the women in our own group suggested we start the day by convening after breakfast to sing the Communist anthem "The Internationale" and then make the day's plans. Unfortunately, the plan didn't work, since we found it almost impossible to get breakfast served to us. To get anything to eat, we had to come into the coffee shop no more than two at a time, since a large group would be completely ignored. The government, by instructing its workers that their revolutionary duty prohibited accepting tips, took away all incentive to serve, since their salary got them virtually nothing. I was reminded of the old *New Yorker* cartoon where a sign in a coffee shop says, "Tipping is considered an insult," while a box stands on the counter with the label, "Deposit insults here."

Over and over throughout the junket, we saw workers accepting dreadful working conditions without any perceptible complaints. One day our group went to the refrigerator factory at Santa Clara, which we were told produced four hundred units a day. The air in the plant was fetid, stinking of fumes and chemicals. The appliances were built with fiberglass insulation, and the workers wore no masks or protective devices to prevent them from inhaling the noxious fumes and fibers, which we knew could potentially cause cancer. The fiberglass residue was so heavy that it came down like snowfall. When we told the manager of our concern over the lack of protection afforded the workers, he told us, "If it were dangerous, Fidel would have informed us. Masks would cut down production, and we are certain that what we are doing is safe."

In Havana, we were taken to the famous Partagas cigar factory, originally built in 1905. Cigars were still rolled and manufactured by hand in the old manner; only one room was mechanized. The quality of the cigar, we were told, was dependent upon the old techniques of curing and treating the tobacco.

The union representative said that the central economic board set quotas for production, and these goals had to be met. Here I received my education in the reality of socialist economics. What if workers felt that the quota was far too high and they could not produce the amount of cigars required? I asked. The union rep's answer was that the party's economists knew what was needed, and it was the workers' responsibility to meet the revolution's goals. If they could not fulfill their task working Monday through Friday, they would have to come in on weekends.

The most telling event on our trip, however, was our tour of the Havana General Psychiatric Hospital. We started with a display of "before and after" pictures. Old photos from the 1930s and '40s showed a facility akin to that in the famous movie *Snake Pit*, with mental patients herded together in unimaginably grotesque fashion. Now, the hospital was the revolution's pride and joy, a showcase of what socialism could achieve. Groups of patients lived in small, comfortable, individual units; others were in clean wards with simple Danish Modern furniture. The hospital was on spacious, manicured grounds, and even had its own baseball team and stadium. We all agreed: if we were confined to a mental hospital, we would definitely prefer that facility to, let's say, New York City's Bellevue Hospital.

Still, our meeting with the head doctor and his staff was not reassuring. First, we were told (by a doctor who spoke flawless English) that individuals were committed through a new kind of test, an evaluation of paintings they were asked to make, which the doctor said indicated their mental state, and also by a new technique of reading fingerprints, which he assured us showed their true state of mental development at the time they were taken. When we toured the arts center, I saw an obviously energetic and totally sane young man teaching patients how to paint. He seemed to know English, so I asked him how he was able to deal with those patients who were clearly mentally unbalanced. He laughed nervously and replied, "I'm a patient myself." I didn't understand. Then he said, "I'm a homosexual, and that is why I'm confined here." An artist, he passed the time by using his skills to help others in the arts and crafts unit. When we confronted the doctor during the question and answer period, he argued that homosexuality was a disease justifying commitment to a mental hospital.

As the tour progressed, we couldn't help but notice the obvious glazed and drugged-out expression on the faces of most of the patients. Clearly they had been given massive doses of tranquilizers, but when we asked the doctor in charge about it, we heard an even more shocking answer. "We are proud," he told us, "that in our institution, we have a larger proportion of hospital inmates who have been lobotomized than any other mental hospital in the world." Lobotomy, he assured us, did wonders for their behavior and state of well-being. Indeed, he told us that a huge percentage of those incarcerated were in fact recipients of these lobotomies. We were flabbergasted, particularly a young man named Larry, a radical therapist who taught at a New Jersey college. "This stinks!" Larry screamed to our group as we got back on our bus. "Lobotomy is a horror. We must do something to stop this. It's exactly what we're working against at home." Castro loyalist Suzanne Ross glared at Larry, shot us all a contemptuous look, and said harshly, "We have to understand that there are differences between capitalist lobotomies and socialist lobotomies."

As we continued on our tour, the differences among us became more pronounced. Once, we got into a heated debate about the Soviet invasion of Czechoslovakia in 1968, which Castro supported on the grounds of solidarity with the Soviet Union. His justification, I argued, was opportunistic and unconvincing. The response of most of the group was heated: I was a counter-revolutionary, a reactionary, and worst of all, a racist. Cole, who was white, and Bambera and another black woman in our group, whose name I do not recall, said, "How could you care about the plight of white European Czechs, when U.S. imperialism is supporting the oppression of blacks in Mozambique and Portugal?" Moreover, others argued, to criticize Castro and support opponents of the Soviet Union was to endanger the continued survival of the Cuban Revolution. I was also castigated for signing a petition by American leftist dissenters demanding an end to political repression in the Soviet Union, and offering support to the struggle of the new Soviet dissidents. The ad, they argued, aided the CIA and American imperialism.

We stayed in Cuba for more than a month, and despite our constant arguments, we saw and learned a lot. Yet although I had trouble admitting it to myself, the net effect was to make me start to rethink my most fervently held assumptions. It was an accumulation of small things that began to push doubts into the forefront of my thinking. I had looked forward, for instance, to our meeting with the revolution's single most approved cultural figure at the time, the writer Roberto Fernandez Retamar, who was editor in chief of the nation's literary journal, *Casa de las Americas*. By the time our visit took place, Castro had already imprisoned the poet Heberto Padilla, who after serving five weeks in prison in March and April of 1972 appeared before the Writers' Union, where he read a "confession" of his wrongdoings, which the government published and circulated around the world. This was too reminiscent of Stalin's purge trials, and promptly garnered the condemnation of some of the revolution's most avid friends abroad. Eventually, Padilla was allowed to go into exile in the United States.

I was disappointed to find that Retamar, although personally charming, fully defended the revolution's treatment of Padilla. He knew how to appeal to the sensibilities of types like myself, Western intellectuals who might be able to swallow their doubts after hearing the revolution defended by his own authenticity. "I too am concerned about the revolution's mechanical attempt to impose socialist realism," he told us. He claimed to have personally told Castro, "I know nothing about guerrilla warfare, and would not dare suggest how such a struggle be conducted; you know nothing about writing a poem, and therefore you cannot tell me how to do that." This sounded defiantly independent, but then Retamar continued to voice his approval of Castro's belief that the intellectual's task was to help the revolution achieve its goals. That, he said, meant a total reorientation of the artist's view of himself. The example he gave us was most telling. "If I lived in New York," he said with a straight face, "I would smoke marijuana. Perhaps under communism, we will be able to do that here in Cuba. But for now, the revolution cannot permit it." Smoking dope, a key item in the "personal is political" repertory of the radical counterculture and the political New Left back home, was counterrevolutionary in Cuba, where the revolution needed to instill discipline.

After Retamar announced his position on marijuana, I was struck by the behavior of our tour leader, Sandy Levinson. In the Nacional, where we all stayed, Sandy had her own suite, where she received a fresh shipment of flowers and rum every day, as well as a car and driver which were at her constant disposal. It was evident that she also had a fresh stash of grass supplied to her regularly, which she was allowed to smoke in her own room and offer to Cubans, particularly writers and artists, whom she invited up to the suite for a toke or two. A couple of times, I went to speak to Sandy in her suite and found her with prominent Cuban intellectuals who were, to put it simply, stoned out of their minds. Smoking dope, we had been told, was counterrevolutionary and illegal in Communist Cuba, a mark of the most decadent bourgeois lifestyle. Yet here was Sandra Levinson, one of America's most prominent defenders of Castro, corrupting his countrymen with demon weed in her revolutionary salon.

Upon my return home, I decided to write an account of what I had seen and learned. My intention was to offer a view that would support the revolution and oppose U.S. animosity towards it, while suggesting that the revolution would only be strengthened by discarding its repressive practices. Seeking a publication for such an article, I turned to *Liberation,* the libertarian socialist/pacifist magazine edited by David Dellinger. He had been a featured speaker and organizer of the Mobe rallies, and was pictured on the cover of *Life,* marching with the radical Yale historian Staughton Lynd in an antiwar demonstration, splattered with blood and eggs by furious supporters of the war. I selected *Liberation* because, although it was part of the Movement, it was open to those who were generally critical—from a leftist perspective—of Communist ideology and repression.

As a result of my article, which I called "Cuba: A Personal Report," the magazine was flooded with more letters than it had ever received, almost all of it bitterly hostile. "There is some good in everything," one reader wrote. "The blockade [of Cuba] kept the intellectual paws of Professor Ronald Radosh off the Cuban people for fifteen years." And the Marxist-Leninist historian Philip S. Foner declared that my article was valuable "only as demonstrating how a narrow prejudice against any form of Socialism which does not adhere to rituals of men like Radosh blinds such people to the realities of historical, revolutionary developments." What I heard, in short, was the old cry of the 1930s: no enemies on the left!

In a following issue of *Liberation,* all the other members of the group, with the exception of two who agreed with me, issued their own comment: "Some of Us Had a Different Trip." I was arrogant, they wrote, for daring to criticize the "first Free Territory of America." Cuba, they argued, had the democratic values we in the United States only talked about. "For all its flaws," they wrote, the revolution was a "profound and beautiful reality." And because Soviet aid allowed it to exist, it was the duty of North Americans who supported the revolution to refrain from criticizing the Soviet Union. To engage in anti-Soviet remarks served only one purpose: to detract "from the fight against U.S. imperialism."

The collapse of the United States Embassy in Saigon and the victory of Ho Chi Minh in 1975 brought relief to those weary of the war, and cheers from those of us who always savored the long-awaited victory of the Vietcong. Watching the sad videos of the helicopters departing from the building near the embassy, with thousands of Vietnamese trying helplessly to get aboard, our response then was utter happiness. We had won in Vietnam! The Vietnamese people would now have their long-fought-for national independence and would proceed to build socialism. Soon after, when Pol Pot's brutal forces overthrew the Lon No regime in Cambodia and began the evacuation of the cities and the murder of thousands of their own countrymen, we again cheered. On a trip to Boston, Allis and I stayed at the home of her friend Emily Schatzow, who was then going out with Danny Shechter, the radical newscaster on the leading rock station, WBCN, who called himself "Danny Shechter, the news dissector." Shechter told us about visiting Cambodia for his station and seeing all the corrupt members of the *ancien régime* trembling before the fighting spirit of the forces led by Pol Pot. When Cambodia fell, Shechter wore a T-shirt with the slogan "We Won in Vietnam and Cambodia."

Back home, the first Sunday after the war's end, the antiwar movement gathered for an impromptu rally in Central Park, where so many of our marches had taken place. Allis and I stood in the front, watching Joan Baez and Phil Ochs sing "The War Is Over," a ballad Ochs had written years earlier. Then it had been a dream; now his song was an anthem of success. Baez sang all her favorites; she was, after all, the diva of the antiwar movement, the artist who stood alongside the young Bob Dylan and epitomized the union of art and politics. Her husband at the time, David Harris, had even gone to jail for draft resistance, and Joanie herself had gone to Vietnam in solidarity as American bombs fell around her. That, of course, did not help her later, when she circulated a petition condemning the repressive Hanoi regime's atrocities and gross abuse of human rights, which were causing refugees to flee in rickety boats; Joan's old allies crucified her as an "enemy of the people."

In truth, the end of the war produced a great void. Demonstrating, writing articles against the war, marching scores of times to the nation's capital had become the focus of our lives. Some of us had thought we could tie the antiwar movement to a broader movement fighting to change the system; others thought the movement could serve as the vehicle to recruit cadre for a socialist revolutionary party; still others thought the revolution would be cultural and had abandoned politics for dope and rock and roll. But the war had been the center of everything, and now it was gone. None of us admitted it, but we almost all looked inside ourselves with a rising sense of panic and wondered, "What now?"

Party Lines

The mid-1970s was for many of my old comrades a time of confusion. The great cause of Vietnam, the cause of a lifetime, had receded, leaving the Movement like a beached whale on the shores of America—which, now that the war was over, could no longer so easily be called *Amerika*. The idea of an immediate, no-fault revolution, a fantasy of the previous decade, was no longer tenable. We would not break on through to the other side, as in the Doors' revolutionary anthem, or at least not overnight as we had hoped. It was a time when some of my old comrades went looking for love in all the wrong places—human potential movements, therapeutic ecstasies, and personality cults—while others began the long march through the institutions. And I, desperately afraid that my god would fail, went looking for another party to join, communism having long since withered away for me.

While thrashing about for direction, I briefly saw light in the form of a then relatively unknown radical from the West Coast who had moved east. Michael Lerner had been part of the New Left, and more to the point, had been indicted for conspiracy in Seattle in the early 1970s as part of a radical group called the Seattle Eight. The trial gave him the cachet necessary to try starting a new movement. His brief moment came after the publication of his book *The New Socialist Revolution* in 1973.

Lerner eventually got his fifteen minutes of fame as the guru behind Hillary Clinton's "politics of meaning." Back in the Seventies, however, he was less touchy-feely and more narrowly Marxist, often crudely so. Lerner wanted a real socialist revolution, not an anemic American version of the Swedish welfare state. Nor did he want the "bureaucratic" socialism of the Soviet Union and its Eastern European satellite states. He also rejected the New Left's romanticizing of Third World revolutionary movements, although he personally continued to heap praise on Ho Chi Minh and the Vietnamese Communists. He endorsed the "revolutionary violence" used by "the North Vietnamese whose open espousal of and participation in violent struggle has in no way diminished their humanity but made it stronger and more definite by sensitizing them." In short, Lerner sought to place socialism on the agenda" in the new decade, creating what he called "a coherent revolutionary socialist position."

That was enough to interest me. I could ignore Lerner's chapter on how once property relations ended, all societal conflict would disappear. I could ignore his thoughts on how monogamy could be smashed and the "prison" of marriage be made to disappear. (I tended to attribute this to Lerner's vestigial New Leftism, not yet knowing that at his first marriage, the wedding cake bore the inscription "Smash Monogamy.") What moved me was his understanding that we could not wait for a new Trotsky or Lenin to emerge—although some would say that Lerner thought himself to be the Chosen One; I supported his desire to help create "a Socialist party that takes the struggle for political power seriously at every level."

A few weeks after I had read *The New Socialist Revolution*, Michael Lerner was sitting in my living room with a large group of people I had called together, associates of mine from the now collapsed antiwar and radical faculty movements, all anxious to make a new start. I do not remember everyone who came, but I know it included Suzanne Ross, who had made the now famous comment about "socialist lobotomies" in Cuba. It also included Roger Alcaly, a pleasant man I had traveled with to Washington, D.C., for an antiwar protest. At the time, he was the second-ranked squash player in the country, an athlete of great accomplishment, and a committed socialist. As time passed I lost touch with him, and was surprised to find his name later on articles in the *New York Review of Books,* where he was identified as an investment banker and chairman of his own Wall Street firm. In all, about forty or fifty of my friends crowded our living room to hear Lerner give his pitch.

As a result of that meeting, we formed a West Side chapter of Lerner's New American Movement. It was begun, as such things are, with solemn commitment, yet it was clear almost from the beginning that this initiative would amount to little more than a weekly and then a monthly discussion group dealing with topics like the meaning of feminism, the theories of Antonio Gramsci and the prospects for reformed communism (later termed Eurocommunism).

In the meantime, others on the left were not wasting their time. I had always been intrigued with one of them: Michael Harrington, the dynamic leader who emerged from the ranks of Norman Thomas's old Socialist Party to become the face of a youthful, anti-Communist, socialist movement. In my most dogmatic phase, I had disdained him as a member of the reactionary Socialist International, a world movement of right-wing social-democratic parties devoted to misdirecting the working class away from assuming its revolutionary potential. Indeed, years earlier, when Harrington had spoken before our Wisconsin Socialist Club, we greeted him with open hostility. One of our WSC members, Malcolm Sylvers, had even stood up and told him, only half jocularly, "After the revolution, you'll be the first person we line up to be shot."

Harrington started his socialist career as part of the sectarian movement led by Max Shachtman, a disciple of Leon Trotsky who broke with his mentor over the question of the Soviet Union's character. Trotsky believed that Stalin had transformed his revolution into a "deformed worker's state," while Shachtman argued that it had become something far worse, a "bureaucratic collectivist" society in which the state became the new ruling class. That meant change could occur only via a workers' revolution *against* the Soviet leadership, and that under no circumstances—even when the USSR was invaded by the Nazis—could Marxists and revolutionaries give their support to Stalin's regime.

Eventually, as the Cold War developed, Shachtman and his followers moved from viewing the Soviet Union and the United States as moral equivalents, two evil imperialist powers, to viewing the United States in a positive light, since it had a free labor movement and stood for democracy throughout the world. At this point, Harrington broke with his own mentor. In practical politics this meant that in 1972, Harrington would cast his presidential vote for George McGovern, while Shachtman and his followers preferred voting for Richard M. Nixon as a lesser evil than McGovern, whom they regarded as the candidate of anti-Americanism.

The Shachtman group won control of the Socialist Party and soon transformed it into a group they named Social Democrats USA, leaning toward George Meany in the labor movement and toward Senator Henry "Scoop" Jackson of Washington, a defense hawk and Cold War liberal, as their political ally. Meanwhile, Harrington moved to create his own splinter group, which he called the Democratic Socialist Organizing Committee (DSOC), a less heroic name than the Socialist Party, reflecting his expectation that a decade or so of steady organizing was necessary before anything more formidable could emerge.

With turmoil and indecision all around me, I decided to take another look at Harrington. When he announced the founding of his DSOC and scheduled its first convention for October of 1973, Michael Lerner and I decided that it was time to attend and observe what it meant for our own fledgling effort to create a new socialist party. The first person I came across at the meeting was a bona fide member of the radical wing of SDS, Mark Naison. Now a Columbia University graduate student in history, Mark had been a member of the so-called "Mad Dog" faction of SDS, a sect slightly less far-out than the Weathermen. "Why are you here?" I asked, surprised to see him. Mark answered, "I'm tired of being isolated." He wanted to be part of a group of committed socialists with ties to organized labor and grassroots groups.

Hearing Harrington speak in the old McAlpin Hotel ballroom, where his convention took place, I was amazed to find that he came off as a serious Marxist revolutionary. He began by

telling those in attendance, "Today we begin the work of building the Seventies Left." If not exactly as grandiose as "We shall
now proceed to construct the socialist order," Lenin's statement
at the Winter Palace after the Bolshevik seizure of power in 1917,
it at least put his new, more modest agenda in historical context.
What Harrington proposed was in fact that radicals "go where
the people are," meaning into the ranks of the Democratic Party.
He sought nothing less than a "conscious, visible presence" in
the pary by an alliance of New Politics middle-class liberals, the
antiwar movement, radical youth, and the social-democratic Left
of the labor movement, represented primarily by the followers
of Walter Reuther in the United Auto Workers. He would soon
attain that presence with what he called the "socialist caucus"
in Congress, composed of figures like Ron Dellums (California),
John Conyers (Michigan), and other like-minded left-wing
Democrats.

I came away from the convention deeply impressed. I knew
that Harrington was opposed to our own preferred path, that of
creating a new socialist party. Instead, he thought socialism
would grow alongside liberalism, of which it had to be part.
While I criticized Harrington as a man with a "bureaucratic con-
ception of socialism," an adherent of the stale concept of "European social democracy," and worst of all, someone who failed to
challenge "the hierarchical nature of capitalist society," I was glad
that on foreign policy he was not an automatic defender of the
United States. After the coup against the Allende government
in Chile by General Augusto Pinochet, Harrington issued a militant denunciation of the action and blamed the United States
for its complicity. He had, I wrote at the time, clearly rejected
"the old State Department Socialism that supported United
States policy because it was anti-Communist," and I praised him
for "a bold and unequivocal condemnation of the economic
maneuvers of American imperialism."

For the next year or thereabouts, while Harrington organized
and began to gather attention, our New American Movement
(NAM) chapter floundered with little support, no growth, and
weekly discussion groups that never managed to reach beyond
our own small ranks. It was the story of all minor socialist sects.

We spoke to each other, ignored those with whom we disagreed, and were content in our "correct," Gramscian understanding of "capitalist hegemony."

So it was probably only a matter of time before I would swallow my pride and call Harrington at DSOC headquarters. He suggested that we meet for lunch at the old Cedar Tavern, a famous Village hangout frequented by artists and musicians. I was nervous about getting close to someone I had always suspected of being a sellout; but as everyone who had come in contact with Mike knew, was a man of great warmth, as adept at putting his adversaries at ease with his charm as he was at putting them down with his withering wit. Mike understood all the theoretical and political issues we were grappling with, and he was candid and up front about our differences.

"Look," he told me over a burger and fries, "I too want socialism in America. But my argument is simply that we can't obtain it until we first forge an alliance within the mainstream of American liberalism. We can push liberalism to its limits, and be straightforward and open about our socialist critique which the liberals don't share." As much as I hoped that building a new socialist party was the only way to nirvana, I had to agree that he had a point. "Moreover," Mike continued, "we can accept as members people like yourself, even though you might have a different estimate of the Soviet Union." We began to discuss the nature of the New Left, its promise and its limitations, and found that on most points we actually saw eye to eye. And now that Harrington favored withdrawal from Vietnam and had strongly condemned the U.S.-backed coup in Chile, nothing was stopping me from coming aboard.

At the end of lunch, I told Harrington that I would join DSOC. We went up to their nearby rented office space, where he introduced me to Jack Clark, a young man from Boston who had been part of his faction in the Socialist Party fight and was now committed to running the DSOC on a day-to-day basis. Later, Clark would introduce me to another of Harrington's old comrades, Deborah (Debbie) Meier, later to be well known as a major force in American education and founder of the alternative public school in East Harlem, which received worldwide attention from educational reformers. Meier owned a beautiful brownstone in the Upper West Side of Manhattan, in the 70s near Broadway, and Clark lived in one of the bedrooms. Meier's spacious living room would be the center of most New York DSOC meetings, as well as numerous parties, fundraising gatherings, and meetings with European visitors.

I do not remember the exact date when Mike introduced me to Irving Howe, but it was soon after I had joined his organization. Howe, already considered one of the great literary critics and perhaps America's best known and most highly regarded socialist intellectual, had started *Dissent* magazine in 1954, and would serve as its editor and inspiration until his death in 1993. Like Harrington, Howe was interested in an opening to the Left, but was more cautious. After a few months of activity in DSOC, I was nominated to the group's National Board, its governing authority. Howe led an active fight against me, arguing that I had been too close to the Communist movement and that my real agenda was not fully understood. On some level, he probably thought I was infiltrating their ranks in order to pull away cadre for some pro-Soviet splinter group. Despite his opposition, the majority of board members voted in my favor, and I joined the DSOC leadership. Eventually, as it became clear that I had moved into the ranks of democratic socialists, Howe would ask me to join the editorial board of *Dissent,* which meant that I became deeply involved in setting the tone for the nation's major democratic-socialist intellectual journal.

Working for incremental change in a serious political movement was quite a different affair from running to rallies and sit-ins, getting arrested, facing tear gas at Washington, D.C., demonstrations, and the like. Usually it amounted to endless rounds of boring meetings, where different factions in the organization debated topics of the day, such as whether to change the committee into a formal movement, which was done finally in 1982, when the organization merged with NAM to form the Democratic Socialists of America (DSA). But until that moment, DSOC kept trying to develop new strategies for influencing the Democratic Party.

In 1976, Harrington created a front group he called Democratic Agenda, meant to include both liberals and socialists in a new left-wing pressure group within the Democratic Party. Maurice Isserman writes that our "3000 or so activists had managed to play a role in the Democratic Party roughly commensurate to that of the 300,000 strong American Conservative Union within the Republican Party." True or not, in effect it meant holding a long weekend meeting in the nation's capital in February 1976, where we heard speakers like Congresswoman Bella Abzug, the future notorious mayor of Washington, D.C., Marion Barry, and other political luminaries. Harrington condemned Jerry Brown and Michael Dukakis as "neoliberals" who deserted the liberal democratic agenda. One thing that Harrington achieved affected the future of the Left in the 1990s: forging new ties with the public employee unions such as AFSCME, and some old industrial unions such as the International Association of Machinists. Indeed, the IAM's chief, William Winpinsinger (Wimpy, as he was called) declared himself also to be a socialist, and became a vice chair of DSOC.

When Jimmy Carter received the presidential nomination of the Democratic Party, Harrington was at first furious. As we watched the convention in Debbie Meier's living room, he roared with laughter at the famous incident when Ted Kennedy, standing by Carter's side at the podium, reluctantly shook his hand. Kennedy, he laughed, was acting according to Lenin's dictum: "He's supporting Carter like a hangman's rope supports a condemned man." Yet once the nomination was over, Mike gave his full support to Carter and tried to get his administration to back the Humphrey-Hawkins Full Employment Bill, a piece of legislation mandating that the government coordinate economic policies to achieve the old socialist goal of "full employment." (When this finally did occur, in the Reagan Eighties, it was not due to socialist measures, but to economic growth.) For Mike, any bill that held out full employment as a "right" was socialist in content. Later, when Carter undertook economic measures that led Arthur M. Schlesinger Jr. to call him "the most Republican President since McKinley," Mike would again convene a Washington meeting and lead a picket line to the Capitol steps to protest Carter's sellout.

Anyone who knew Mike could not help but be influenced by his charisma, warmth and brilliance. Towards the end of the decade, Allis and I had the chance to travel with him on a political tour of Jamaica at the invitation of Michael Manley, the socialist prime minister of that Caribbean country. During an intense, two-week trip, our small group had a chance to see Mike Harrington at his best. He showed indefatigable energy in touring the country, engaging in lengthy discussions with political leaders ranging from conservative opponents of Manley to the prime minister and other government leaders, and getting to know his travel mates. On one blistering hot day, as we took a swimming break at the pool of the luxury Kingston Sheraton, Mike stood poolside in his swim trunks, beer in hand, and gestured at the beauty of our surroundings, saying, "I'll go wherever the class struggle takes me."

The Jamaican excursion was a combination of political tour and vacation in paradise. As guests of the prime minister, we were given the red-carpet treatment. We also got to see solid evidence of the severe problems facing the country. At the hotel, we were all accosted by a man who called himself "Jesse, the sheriff." For the first time, I came to understand the meaning of the reggae song "Who Shot the Sheriff?" Any two-bit hustler in Jamaica who had a little authority could dub himself sheriff. In this case, the obviously well-connected man seemed to have two main jobs: procuring prostitutes for foreign guests at the luxury hotels, and supplying ganja to locals and tourists. Indeed, Jesse informed us that his birthday party was coming up, that we were all invited, and that most of the top government ministers would also be coming. We wanted to go, but after Harrington thought it over, his revolutionary puritanism got the better of him, and he insisted that we all should decline the invitation. One day, as I was sitting by the pool during a late afternoon break from our work, a scraggly, unkempt man sat down next to me. With his torn clothes and wooly dreadlocks, he looked out of place, to say the least, at the Kingston Sheraton. Allis and I wondered how he managed to get beyond security. He nodded hello and smiled at us, then ordered a drink and sat listening to the hotel's amateurish reggae group. After half an hour, an announcement came out of the hotel's loudspeaker: "Will Bob Marley please come to the front desk." The disheveled stranger got up and walked towards the hotel lobby. Following him, I saw Jesse the self-proclaimed sheriff selling Marley his regular supply of ganja. Marley then left and walked to his car, a white BMW with a license plate proclaiming "BMW."

My efforts in DSOC, however, veered away from the political and towards the intellectual. With over three thousand members, DSOC was able to start its own publication, *Democratic Left,* a monthly newsletter meant to expand the group's visibility to the broader liberal-left movements. But the newsletter remained a small-circulation publication, reaching mainly DSOC members, and hardly known outside of our own circles. Its influence in the literary and political communities was negligible.

I offered to write a regular column, which I called "What's LEFT to Read?" It was meant to be partly a review of literature, books and periodicals, partly an assessment of intellectual currents on the left. Looking back at the issues years later, I was pleased to find that in the February 1980 number, I had singled out for praise the December 9 issue of *The Nation,* which featured a look at the Left by my old friend David Horowitz, tracing his disillusionment with outworn Marxist premises and accusing the Left of being trapped in a romantic vision of politics and of applying a political and moral double standard. Horowitz's essay, I wrote, "is MUST reading," and I said that his question about whether the Left could take a hard look at itself, its critiques, goal and failures, was essential to our movement.

In the February 1981 issue, I decided to review Tom Hayden's latest book, *The American Future: New Visions Beyond Old Frontiers.* Hayden, by then married to Jane Fonda, was becoming a power in the California Democratic Party and assuming a position of national importance. I had always been wary of him, although certainly friendlier to him than was Irving Howe, who in his bitter debate with Hayden years earlier had called the young SDS founder a would-be Lenin or Stalin, and quipped, in a widely repeated remark, "Hayden gives opportunism a bad name." I praised Hayden for joining the movement "to challenge corporate power," but criticized him for calling his movement "economic democracy" rather than socialism, and for taking cheap shots at the views of people like Mike Harrington.

One day when the phone rang at home, I was shocked to hear a voice saying, "Is this Ron? It's Tom." "Tom who?" I replied. "Tom Hayden. I have to get together with you."

I arranged a meeting in DSOC's new Union Square head-quarters. He arrived a few minutes after I got there, and appeared nervous. We went into a vacant room that contained some chairs and a desk. I sat in one of the chairs, but Hayden chose to sit on the desk so he could tower above me as he spoke. I soon found out what he wanted. "You have to repudiate your review," he said. "It's hurt me tremendously. Please write another review, saying you've reconsidered and that you love the book." I was stunned, to put it mildly. I had written what I thought was a friendly and supportive criticism that praised Hayden and his work, and only criticized his antisocialist tirade. But Hayden kept reiterating that it wasn't fair, that I had hurt any chances of his book being read, and that I should immediately write another review. At one point he got on the phone and placed a call to his editor at the publishing house. "I'm here with Ron Radosh," he told the editor. "Please talk to him and get him to write another review."

Here he was, married to Jane Fonda, the subject of nation-wide publicity, a major figure in California politics—and now, begging me to redo a review that perhaps a few hundred people had read. After another hour or so of talking, we shook hands and parted. I did not see Hayden again until 1989, and then only by accident. On my way to meet David Horowitz and Peter Collier in Poland for the "Second Thoughts" conference they had scheduled in Cracow, I found Hayden sitting next to me in the van taking us from the Dulles main terminal to the international airport. I told him that I was on my way to Eastern Europe, well aware that he and Jane Fonda had just been to Prague and other former Soviet satellite states then in ferment, where large crowds and publicity followed them. "I was just there," he said. "They're building a new Left." I had to stop myself from asking him if he was out of his mind.

In the 1970s, as part of Harrington's brief dream of bringing the remnants of the Old Left into a broad socialist movement, there was an overture to Dorothy Healey, a leading ex-Communist from Southern California who had become somewhat of a legend for her willingness to admit the horrors of Stalinism, and who now adhered to the Eurocommunist fantasy. As part of this feeling-out process, Dorothy agreed to come to New York for a friendly debate with Mike Harrington. Allis and I put her up in our apartment, where we talked the entire evening. Dorothy had resigned from the Communist Party in July of 1973, and still had the old party habits. When I teased her about the prospect of joining with DSOC in common endeavors, she responded somewhat testily, "I certainly don't relish belonging to any group that harbors loyalists of the Second International."

Trying to cheer her up, I said to Dorothy, "Well, at least the Red-baiters were wrong about the CP getting Moscow gold." (Of course, the files found in Moscow by Harvey Klehr and John Haynes after the breakup of the Soviet Union have yielded definitive proof that as late as the Gorbachev era, the Soviets readily sent millions to Gus Hall to finance his miniscule movement.) Dorothy's response to my quip virtually stunned me. "No, you're wrong. How do you think the CP bought its building on West Twenty-third Street?" She then told me—but managed to leave out of her own 1990 autobiography, *Dorothy Healey Remembers a Life in the American Communist Party*—that on one of her last trips to Moscow for the party, she was given a suitcase filled with thousands of dollars to smuggle into America, to be used by the CPUSA as it saw fit. Party leaders had used the money to buy their piece of prime Manhattan real estate for a headquarters. When I put this tidbit into a review of her book for the *American Spectator*, Dorothy wrote a letter denying this and threatening to sue. My wife, who was present at the conversation, verified the story. Moreover, I told Dorothy that if she did sue, I would put into print all the other things she had indiscreetly told me.

As for Harrington, an indication of how far he had come in his effort to integrate a socialist vision into the liberal wing of the Democratic Party came at the 1980 convention in Madison Square Garden. DSOC set up shop there in its own name and was awarded floor passes for its members. I sat with Mike and others listening to the major speech given by Ted Kennedy, whom we regarded as the Democratic Party's best hope, the titular leader of the broad left wing. I proudly handed out leaflets to Democratic delegates, explaining to them that we were not only Democrats but also socialists, and that our work would only strengthen their ability to reach their own liberal goals. For us, the highlight of the convention was a meeting Harrington scheduled in DSOC's name at one of the convention hotels, billed as the first meeting of "the socialist caucus of the Democratic Party." Harrington presided over talks by William Winpinsinger, Ron Dellums and John Conyers. The New York television news was in attendance, and we even got some network coverage. As the Seventies came to an end, like Mike Harrington, I was certain that socialism was in our nation's future.

Those of us in Harrington's socialist movement had one great fear: if Ronald Reagan was elected president, the nation would head towards extreme reaction, if not fascism. Speaking to students at New York University, Harrington warned them that this presidential election was the most critical in decades. If one considered only what a Reagan presidency would mean for the people of Central America who were demanding their freedom, from El Salvador to Nicaragua, Harrington told them, the issue was clear. As backwards as Jimmy Carter had been, he was highly preferable to Ronald Reagan.

Gathered at Debbie Meier's on election eve, we watched the incoming returns with trepidation. It was soon obvious to us that Americans had once again voted the wrong way. As the results became evident, one of the more sober and conservative members of our movement, Alex Spinrad, shocked us by saying quite appropriately that even if we did not like the vote, American democracy had worked. "The people have spoken," Spinrad said, "and it is the greatness of our country that we live in a democratic system where a free election determines who governs us."

He went on to propose that we toast to Ronald Reagan, in the hope that he would govern well. Alex's own glass was the only one raised.

My Rosenberg Case and Theirs

IN MY YOUTH THE PASSION OF JULIUS AND ETHEL ROSENBERG WAS the great cause that wedded me to the Left. Ironically, discovery of what that cause had actually meant thirty years later was the event that began my slow-motion exit from the Left. I had started paying revived attention to the Rosenberg case back in the early 1970s, the time that the couple's two sons, Michael and Robert Meeropol, had made their identities public and began a campaign to vindicate their parents. As soon as I heard about their decision, I immediately offered to join them in the new group they were establishing, the National Committee to Re-Open the Rosenberg Case. In addition to serving justice, I saw the case as offering me an opportunity to tie my past and present together.

In the years since the Rosenbergs' martyrdom, it never crossed my mind that there was the slightest chance that the Rosenbergs might be guilty of what J. Edgar Hoover called "the crime of the century." It became an article of faith, not just for me but for the Left generally, that Julius and Ethel Rosenberg were the victims of a government-sponsored conspiracy. And in the backwash of the historical revisionism touched off by the war in Vietnam, this conviction became all the firmer and more sacrosanct.

Years after the Rosenbergs' execution, a spate of books appeared that attempted to prove that they were victims of a government frame-up. Only one made an impact, because of its scholarly veneer, its strong narrative, and its use of the techniques of investigative reporting. Written by Walter and Miriam Schneir, *Invitation to an Inquest* appeared in 1965, and the reviewer for the *New York Times* welcomed it as a "major event in the history of the celebrated case." The Schneirs began their work after other books questioning the prosecution, the death sentence and the verdict had already been published, but their presentation of the case as a monstrous conspiracy was the most effective yet. Central to their argument was the testimony of Harry Gold, the key prosecution witness in the case. The Schneirs' startling revelation was that Gold, who had claimed to have traveled to Albuquerque, New Mexico, to retrieve atomic data from Julius Rosenberg's brother-in-law David Greenglass, had been lying. The evidence presented in court to prove that he had made such a trip, a Hilton Hotel card, had been forged. Since for many readers, the Schneirs had destroyed the validity of that evidence, the government's case was in their eyes proven to be a fraud.

Like others emotionally involved with the case, I had read the Schneirs' book with admiration and delight: finally, so many years after the execution, the truth had come out. For many of us, the book was definitive. In 1975, filmmaker Alvin Goldstein produced a PBS documentary based on the book, reiterating their thesis for a vast television audience. In an introduction to a book based on the script, civil libertarian Nat Hentoff, a self-proclaimed "anti-Stalinist and anti-all-authoritarianism," said that the Schneirs' argument convinced him the Rosenbergs "were being tried *because* of their political beliefs—or what the state considered to be their political beliefs." Like others who had gone through the stormy Sixties, Hentoff, whose views were now colored by Vietnam and the other fights of the decade, wrote that the U.S. government had been "made paranoid by the Cold War" and hoped the people would see that "their government would 'protect' them against spies"; for this reason, "those two corpses" would be considered proof of a putative "Communist menace." So powerful was Goldstein's television documentary, thought Hentoff, that along with the Schneirs' book it might provide the "significant breakthrough" to proving that a heinous crime against the Rosenbergs had been committed.

The stakes were high. For if the Rosenbergs were innocent, the Old Left was correct: America had been on the edge of fascism, and it was the United States, not the Soviet Union, that threatened the peace and sought to repress those who believed in freedom and democracy. There had been no conspiracy of spies. The Communists were just another group of "dissenters" who posed no more threat to American national security than the Soviet Union did to the American national interest. When Michael and Robert Meeropol finally sued the United States government under the terms of the Freedom of Information Act (FOIA) for release of all FBI files pertaining to the case, I assumed along with them that this material would provide the vindication we all had been predicting.

"It all comes back to Watergate," Robert had said. In other words, this crime against America was just a repeat of what the government had done to his parents, and to the Left they had believed. Like Michael and Robbie, I believed that the disillusion caused by Watergate and the Nixon presidency had prepared the American public to reevaluate what always was a political case. And so, week in and week out, I attended executive committee meetings of the Committee to Re-Open the Rosenberg Case, usually held in the West Side of Manhattan at the apartment of Abbot Simon, an executive who had been a leader of the Young Communist League in the 1940s.

Around this time, I ran into friend and political associate James Weinstein, who by then had started a new socialist newspaper in Chicago, *In These Times.* Jim was in New York, and I had lunch with him. Recently, Jim had seen my old friend David Horowitz in California, and had discussed with him why he knew that the Rosenbergs were not innocent. David had informed me of this conversation and suggested that I ask Jim about it. I began my discussion with Jim by telling him how happy I was to be involved in a new campaign to exonerate the Rosenbergs. His reply stunned me. "Be careful," he said. "There's more to it than you know. I have some knowledge of what really happened and it isn't what you think." I pressed him to explain. He reluctantly said he would tell me of an experience he had shortly before the Rosenbergs were arrested.

During the academic year of 1948–49, Jim Weinstein and his roommate, Max Finestone, were both seniors at Cornell

University and active members of the university's Communist Party chapter. Sometime in the middle of the school year, Jim said, Finestone told him that he was quitting the party to undertake "secret work." Weinstein had no idea what his friend was up to; he knew enough not to inquire about details. At the same time, Finestone got a job working for a small contracting business in Ithaca run by a man named Al Sarant, an engineer who had attended CCNY with Julius Rosenberg and who eventually would flee to the Soviet Union, where he and his partner, Joel Barr, would develop the Soviet defense industry's capability in microtechnology.

Jimmy told me that Max would often borrow his car, a 1940 Buick convertible. He assumed that Finestone was using it to visit his parents, who had a nearby farm in upstate New York, although there was the possibility that he was actually using it somehow for his "secret work." Jim forgot about all this by June 1949 when he graduated, moved back to New York City, and entered Columbia University Law School. That fall, however, he took a weekend trip to Ithaca and stayed at the Finestone farm. At the end of the weekend, Max asked him to give someone a lift back to the city. That "someone" was a plain-looking man with a moustache and glasses, introduced to him only as "Julius." During the long drive back to the city, Jim told me, "Julius" sat in the car's back seat and never said one word. When they arrived at the George Washington Bridge, "Julius" asked to be left off.

Later that fall, Max Finestone moved to the city, first staying at an apartment he rented at 65 Morton Street in Greenwich Village. This apartment would later emerge in the Rosenberg trial as the alleged location where Sarant and Barr photocopied material to be transmitted to the Soviets. Towards the end of December, Jim told me, Finestone phoned to say he had to vacate the premises immediately, and asked to move in with Jim. Within a few days, Max turned up at Jim's apartment, and once again, the two were roommates. As before, Finestone continued to borrow Weinstein's car.

One evening in July 1950, there was a knock on Jim's door at the small East Ninth Street flat. Jim opened the door, and was surprised to find that the person standing there was the same

"Julius" whom he had driven back from Ithaca. He asked Jim if Max was home. When Jim said no, the man replied, "Tell him Julius was here," then turned and departed. When Max came home later that evening, Weinstein mentioned what had happened. Max asked him nervously whether he was sure it was Julius. Jim told Max it was the very same person he had asked him to drive back from Ithaca. At this, Jim told me, "Max turned white as a sheet," and blurted out: "He knows he's not supposed to come here." Jim thought little of it. Then, two weeks later, he looked at the front page of the *Daily News,* the tabloid paper, and saw a larger-than-life photo of Julius Rosenberg and a breaking story about atomic espionage. "I became enraged at Max," Weinstein told me, "because he had moved in with me when he knew the heat was on."

After the Rosenbergs' arrest, Jim Weinstein also told me, he suddenly received notification that he had been expelled from the Communist Party, without any chance of appearing to state his case. Moreover, he learned from friends in the party that they had been told to break off all communication with him and avoid him as completely as possible. For years, Weinstein tried to get back into the party. It was not until after the Rosenbergs' death that he was finally readmitted. "The party wanted nothing to do with an espionage charge," Jim said, "and if it looked like I might be drawn into the case, and even indicted as a spy, they wanted to be able to say that they had expelled me on their own as an untrustworthy element."

At the time Weinstein told me all this, I shrugged it off as interesting but highly speculative. Indeed, I told Jim's story to Michael Meeropol's best friend, the historian Gerald Markowitz, who came to my apartment to hear it. Gerry said he would pass it on to Michael. A week later, he called to say that Michael said "there's nothing to it." I put the whole episode in the back of my mind.

When the announcement was made about the government's decision to release the Rosenbergs' FBI files, my first thought was that I was the perfect person to undertake a serious effort to examine them and write a book. I was a historian, and I was politically reliable. Like the Meeropols, I hoped and expected that the files would provide enough hard data to prove a frame-up, or at least reveal that a major miscarriage of justice had taken place. Indeed, the bits and pieces of material I had seen suggested that this was the case. Documents had already been released revealing illegal *ex parte* communication between the judge and the prosecution, which indicated that the case certainly had its share of tainted government procedures.

At first I thought of writing an article rather than an entire book. Since I wasn't a journalist, I decided to find a collaborator. I turned to an old friend, Sol Stern, a colleague from my University of Iowa graduate school days, and a former *Ramparts* editor and New Left activist. Stern was a smart writer and shrewd political observer, and we shared a common background and perspective. We were both left-wing Jews from New York, for whom the Rosenberg case had been a central concern. Sol was interested in the project, and we decided that we should start by taking a look at the FBI files on the case, which were open for use at the offices of the Meeropols' lawyer, Marshall Perlin.

The first thing that happened when Sol and I began to examine the files was that Jimmy Weinstein's story was confirmed. Reading through the documents, we saw scores of reports given to the FBI by a previously secret informant named Jerome Eugene Tartakow. He was a street hustler and con man who had been arrested for car theft; but he came from a Bronx working-class family, and like Rosenberg, had been a member of the Young Communist League. While Rosenberg was awaiting trial, he found himself sharing a cell with Tartakow in the holding facility in New York, the so-called Tombs. Tartakow realized immediately that his good luck in a prison roommate gave him just the leverage he needed to cut a deal: he would provide the FBI with information about what Rosenberg told him in exchange for being able to leave prison with time served.

Prison informers are notoriously unreliable, and naturally I doubted the veracity of Tartakow's stories. Yet it became clear to me that he gave the bureau information that he could only have learned from Julius Rosenberg. And when agents investigated the leads, they turned up the information necessary for a conviction. The most famous example was a tip that led to a last-minute surprise witness. On the last day of the trial, the Justice Department brought in a neighborhood photographer who testified that shortly before his arrest, Julius and his entire family had come into his store to have passport photos taken. The story confirmed that the Rosenbergs were indeed planning to leave the country on short notice. The government only learned about the photographer, it turned out, because during the trial, Rosenberg told his cellmate that it was a good thing the government didn't know they had passport pictures taken. Tartakow immediately passed this tidbit on. The FBI then combed the neighborhood and easily found the passport photographer, who easily recalled taking their photo.

But what stunned me in reading the FBI files was that the bureau had information about Jim Weinstein's car being used by Max Finestone for the purpose of ferrying Rosenberg around in Ithaca. Tartakow even provided the story—obviously related to him in the prison cell—of how Weinstein had taken Julius back from Ithaca to New York. In one of their last jailhouse conversations, Tartakow told the FBI that Rosenberg had said one of the last men he recruited—alluding to Max Finestone—had a roommate who was a law student and "the son of a wealthy family," a characterization that fit Weinstein, and that this last recruit had borrowed the roommate's black Buick convertible to drive Julius to Ithaca to see Al Sarant. This, of course, was precisely what Jim Weinstein had related to me. This story had come to the FBI via Tartakow, and he could only have learned of it from Rosenberg himself.

Ironically, Tartakow's truthfulness was further confirmed by a lawyer in Marshall Perlin's staff named Bonnie Brower, who let Sol and me know that Julius so trusted Tartakow that upon the informer's release from jail, he arranged for him to work for Emanuel Bloch, the Rosenbergs' counsel. Among other chores, Tartakow drove Bloch and the Rosenbergs' sons up to Sing Sing prison for visits. And, Brower told us, when Tartakow was hired as a driver, he had a recommendation from the Communist Party's chairman, Eugene Dennis. Then she gave us a letter to read, from Tartakow to Emanuel Bloch, dated January 24, 1953, and actually made a photocopy for us bearing the imprint of the Perlin law office.

The letter confirmed the immense trust that the Rosenbergs and their counsel had in this informer and proved that the stories Tartakow related were not fabricated. But once Stern and I began to ask more candid questions about this informer, we suddenly became *personae non gratae* at the Perlin law office. Marshall Perlin abruptly told us that we had to leave. Since we were just beginning our research, this meant we had to travel to Washington, D.C., and rent an expensive hotel room while we used the same files in the FBI's reading room.

The damning Tartakow reports suggested something that I did not particularly want to hear: that the Rosenberg case was morally far more complex than I had always believed. Sol and I knew we had a good story, and we decided to seek a commission to help support further research. We started by calling Ed Klein, then editor in chief of the *New York Times Magazine*. He was quite excited, and after canvassing his editorial board, he gave us a go-ahead. Then we managed to obtain the only interview yet given since his release from prison by David Greenglass, the defendant who turned prosecution witness and testified against his sister and brother-in-law. That alone guaranteed that the piece would get attention. When we finally turned the piece in to Klein, he was ecstatic. He phoned to congratulate us on a job well done; the magazine was scheduling it as the cover story in the issue then being sent to bed. But a few days later, we received a shocking late-night call from Klein. "It's been spiked from above," he told us. "Abe killed it!"

After the magazine's top editor and his entire board had approved the article, A. M. Rosenthal, then the *New York Times'* editor in chief, read it and, without giving us any reasons, ordered that it not be printed. We were stunned. The *Times* had agreed to pay us a large fee for the exclusive article and had paid all of our research expenses, including our stay in Washington, D.C., and the photocopying of thousands of pages of FBI files. Why, at the very last minute, would Abe Rosenthal kill the story? It was especially odd given Rosenthal's strong anticommunism and his own stories centering on Soviet dissidents and repression.

Finally, off the record, one of the magazine's editors explained: "Judge Irving R. Kaufman [the Rosenberg case judge who heard their case and handed down the death sentence] is serving on the U.S. Court of Appeals, and he is generally the justice who sits on freedom of information and press cases." This editor went on to explain that since our article agreed with critics who accused the judge of having engaged in illegal *ex parte* communication during the trial, and since we argued that he was wrong to hand down a death sentence, the *Times* "could not afford to run a piece that might inflame Kaufman to vote against the paper in an important press case."

After this setback, Sol and I began to look for a fallback position. I immediately telephoned Marty Peretz, publisher and editor in chief of the *New Republic*. Marty had contacted me a few years back, after reading a review of mine in *The Nation*, to say that he would love to have me as a contributor. A man who himself had recently begun a sharp turn away from the ranks of the Left, and who was well acquainted with the symbolic importance of the Rosenberg case to the American Left, Peretz immediately agreed to publish the article. We cemented our agreement at a wonderful Chinese meal at David Keh's famous Uncle Tai restaurant, then located in Manhattan's Upper East Side. And so began my long-standing association with TNR, which exists to this day.

Our story appeared first in the June 23, 1979, issue of the *New Republic*. The article, called "The Hidden Rosenberg Case: How the FBI Framed Ethel to Break Julius," was headline news in papers throughout the country; Stern and I were interviewed on the *Today Show*, and *Newsweek* ran a feature article. The Left's reaction provided a lesson in itself. *Seven Days,* a radical newsweekly edited by Dave Dellinger and intended as a left-wing version of *Time* and *Newsweek,* offered an article called "The Rosenbergs Framed Again," in which Bonnie Brower was quoted as saying she had never met us. The article went on to say that in fact Sol and I were enemies of the Left, since we seemed "to believe that Communism in the U.S. and abroad is the primary obstacle to true democratic socialism and a threat which must be fought."

Bonnie Brower later sued us for defamation of character, claiming that our story was a fabrication, that she had not given us any material, and that our story was harming her income and client list. The *New Republic* was forced to hire the famed legal counsel Floyd Abrams to defend us. The decision was handed down on May 21, 1981, in the supreme court of the State of New York, in the case known as *Bonnie Brower vs. The New Republic, Inc., Sol Stern and Ronald Radosh*. Asking the modest sum of $2.5 million, Ms. Brower accused us of engaging in a "bald-faced lie, concocted by them out of whole cloth." What was the lie? Our statement that "when Emanuel Bloch hired Tartakow as his driver, it was with [CP chief Eugene] Dennis' recommendation." Brower claimed that we had attributed this statement to her "deliberately and maliciously" in order to give the FBI inform-ant Tartakow credibility. She then went on to say that she had never "met or spoken with Mr. Radosh in my life." This from a woman who had told Stern and me this fact about Tartakow as she handed us the very letter we used in our article from her office copy machine!

After taking depositions, the court threw the case out and we were vindicated in all eyes, except those looking at us from the Left.

My friends made it clear that they were shocked by what I had done. Even Jim Weinstein, who was responsible for my starting to rethink the case, found himself under the gun for his defense of me. Even then, when I had not even gotten to the middle of my journey, I had come far enough to know that I differed greatly with Jim on the issue of anticommunism, which he abhorred. Jim's problem, as he wrote me, was that he wanted me to show Julius Rosenberg to have been a spy, while at the same time explaining it "sympathetically." In other words, he wanted me to write a book that would show that the Rosenbergs saw their espionage as "entirely in the best interests of the American people"—as if that would excuse it. As Weinstein wrote me, I was beginning to "slip into anti-Communism in the bad sense ... part of an attempt to live down your own political past."

"Even if it's true," another good friend told me, "you shouldn't say this, because you're helping the other side." And others would say, quite bluntly, "The facts are irrelevant. We need the Rosenbergs as heroes." While I was vacationing in Cape Cod, my old Madison friend Roz Baxandall, who had a summer place there, phoned to say, "I want to set up a session here with you and others to engage in self-criticism, so you can see that you shouldn't pursue this book." The *New Republic,* as expected, was inundated with letters to the editor, including one from the left-wing historian Eric Foner, himself a Red-diaper baby, complaining that the article violated all the accepted "canons" of historical scholarship.

Why did these people love the Rosenbergs so? Searching through my files recently, I came across a long personal letter written to me in 1979 by another friend, the historian Mark Naison, then a young professor at Fordham University who had written a pioneering academic study of the Communist Party in Harlem. Naison did not try to impugn my methodology, as did Foner. Rather, he wrote something that explained exactly why the Rosenberg myth was so important to "our crowd." "The Rosenbergs knew how to die; they knew how to sacrifice for their comrades," he wrote me, "even when, as the case may be, they didn't quite know just where the chain of events led. It is no accident that people like this were the ones who fought the Scottsboro battles, built the unions, put their bodies on the line." Indeed, Naison explained, despite their treachery, the Rosenbergs' espionage was "genuinely patriotic," since they did it to better mankind. Finally, Mark left me with a threat: unless I turned away from liberal anticommunism, "you repudiate much of your own scholarly work and gravely compromise your reputation with people of my generation who respect you." If I did not, I would become known as someone who puts "his intellectual tools in the service of the right."

As the furor occasioned by the article passed, Sol and I tried to move ahead with our book, but soon we reached an impasse. To Sol, it seemed that the article had said it all; a book would only expand on what we had already written and not get much attention. We decided it would be better if he left the project. I realized that for a lengthy book on the case, my academic prose would not be sufficient; I still needed a skilled and lively writer, who also had a good sense of history and politics, to help me tell the story.

Assisted by Marian Wood, my editor at Holt, Rinehart and Winston, I set out to audition various authors. I recall phoning Joe Klein, then a young journalist, thinking his status as an independent-minded leftist might make him interested; but he turned me down flat. I asked others to submit samples of writing based on research I turned over to them, but found what they gave me unsatisfactory. Finally, the writer Joel Agee suggested I speak to a good friend of his named Joyce Milton. Much to my pleasure, I learned that she was not only a first-rate writer, but also thoroughly familiar with all the issues in the Rosenberg case, and she had been a college classmate of Michael Meeropol's. We agreed to take a chance on each other. Within a short time, we were on our way.

The book gave us a chance to cover every aspect of the case— not just the dramatic new information about the spy ring put together by Julius Rosenberg, but all the other ramifications of the case. Joyce and I dealt with the nature of the scientific evidence; we presented a full account of various figures in the case including David and Ruth Greenglass, Harry Gold, Max Elitcher and William Perl; and we discussed the trial itself: the government's presentation of its case, the weak defense that the Rosenbergs received, and the role of the judge and the prosecuting team. Most important, we dealt at length with the politics of the case, especially the worldwide propaganda war instituted by the Communist movement and how it played out in the United States.

When we had finished writing *The Rosenberg File* and awaited its publication, we learned that, in a lame attempt to upstage us, Walter and Miriam Schneir had managed to get a new contract to republish their 1965 book with a new introduction. We worried immediately that reviewers and the media would view this as a new research effort, rather than a preemptive strike against

MY ROSENBERG CASE AND THEIRS

us. I brainstormed and had an idea: why not write a long review of their book, using our own material to take on their thesis directly? I called Robert Silvers at the *New York Review of Books,* and he welcomed the idea. The result was a lengthy analysis by Joyce and me in their pages, as well as additional weeks of extensive back-and-forth in the publication's letter pages. Our review not only had the effect of denigrating the Schneirs' research and conclusions, but also created an even larger audience for *The Rosenberg File.*

We knew, judging from the response to the *New Republic* piece, that the book would get attention, but we did not anticipate how much. Indeed, the publisher, Holt, Rinehart and Winston, had not even planned a book tour. They expected the book to do "respectably," as they put it, but not much better than that. The publication date was set for the week after Labor Day in 1983. I was on vacation with my family in Vermont, expecting to be back in New York City before any reaction emerged. But two weeks early, a rave review appeared in the *New York Times,* written by its chief critic, Michiko Kakutani. Soon after, Marian Wood called to tell us that we had the front-page review in the *New York Times Book Review,* in addition to another column about the book in the same publication by Walter Goodman. In his front-page review, Harvard law professor Alan Dershowitz proclaimed that "all future discussions about the Rosenberg case will have to begin with the historical fact that Julius Rosenberg was guilty of espionage."

Dershowitz's review was followed by one major review after another, almost universally positive. The columnist and social critic Max Lerner wrote that "if any book can establish the truth about the whole episode," this was it. Harvard historian Alan Brinkley proclaimed it "an extraordinarily extensive and impressive piece of historical detective work," and went on to say that rather than using the case to "settle old ideological scores," my coauthor Joyce Milton and I had "risen above the passion ... and produced a book of remarkable balance and restraint." The columnist George Will called it "a work of history that also is a historical event." And Allen Weinstein, whose own study of the Hiss case, *Perjury,* had created a similar controversy, noted that we lay "to rest vital elements of the mythologies of left and right about the case."

I was still an active member of Mike Harrington's organization, DSOC, and still considered myself to be a good citizen of the left-wing world. I had naïvely hoped that even though my book established the guilt of Julius Rosenberg, I would not be read out of the Movement. I knew that Communists, members of the Old Left and fellow travelers would not forgive me, but I did not expect a negative reaction from my DSOC comrades. After all, they all denied being pro-Soviet; they themselves were critics of Stalinist communism and had no overriding reason to want to keep the Rosenbergs alive in the nation's memory as innocent victims of a Cold War witch hunt. I was soon to learn otherwise. The first two people I approached for blurbs were Mike Harrington and Irving Howe. Both of them turned me down flat. Howe said simply, "I can't get involved in that," shrugged his shoulders, and walked away. "But Irving, it's important that I have serious people of the Left endorsing the book." "Sorry," he responded. "I don't want anything to do with it." I was stunned. I assumed that of all the people I approached, Irving Howe would be the most sympathetic. He was a relentless opponent of communism in the 1950s, and his own essays on the subject were tough and outspoken. What had happened? I wondered. Howe, for whatever reasons, would not elaborate or answer my queries.

Harrington was more up front. "I always knew they were guilty," he said, "but we're trying to get former Communists who have left the party but are still pro-Soviet into our organization, and I can't do anything to alienate them." I told Mike that this was a matter of truth and history, not contemporary politics, but he wouldn't budge. "I'm willing to say publicly if asked that I don't think your book is a McCarthyite tract," he told me. "But that's all I'll say." The man I had considered a courageous and bold intellectual, a man who repudiated Stalinist modes of thought for a tough radical viewpoint, was saying in effect that although he knew I was correct about the case, the truth had to be subordinated to his present political agenda, which was to get former Communists as his comrades.

When the book was published, I never received an iota of public support from the democratic socialist intellectuals, all of whom seemed deeply embarrassed that I had written *The Rosenberg File*. And of course, the hard Left—the remnants of the New Left, the CP fellow travelers and the "progressives"—were all of one mind: I had become the new enemy. The September 7, 1983, issue of *The Guardian* ran a front-page article titled, "A Falsified 'Rosenberg File.'" My account, wrote the paper's reporter, "stretches the truth so far it breaks," and then he went on to accuse Joyce and me of using "nonexistent FBI documents." He regarded it as an example of "historical fraud and media gullibility, not a work of scholarship." One of the charges he and others made was that a principal figure in the case, an elderly Nashville lawyer named Fyke Farmer, had never given me any material or spoken to me. I had said—as was the case—that Farmer mailed me a complete copy of his Rosenberg case file, photocopied from the material in his office. Farmer told the paper that this was false. Fortunately, when journalist Margot Adler from NPR asked me about this, I was able to show her the very envelope Farmer used, including his letterhead and the actual documents.

The paper quoted an old friend of mine, the historian Blanche Cook—later to become famous for the biography in which she tried to "out" Eleanor Roosevelt as a lesbian—as saying that "Radosh's deliberately obscure citations, which render his documents almost impossible to check, as well as his reliance on anonymous sources, are shocking departures from standard scholarly methods and force me to question his intent and his honesty."

The most scurrilous article appeared in a pamphlet published by the Meeropols' new group, the Fund for Open Information and Accountability. It was written by the Rutgers historian Norman Markowitz, a man who in the twenty-first century still proudly proclaims himself a member of the Communist Party USA. Markowitz wrote, "*The Rosenberg File* conforms to the age-old anti-Semitic stereotype of Jews as disloyal and greedy," and accused me of "apologizing" for anti-Semitism. Evidently because Julius Rosenberg was Jewish and I concluded that he had been guilty of conspiracy to commit espionage, my argument was therefore anti-Semitic. Another scathing attack came, ironically, from a woman who had been a neighbor of mine and a good friend when I lived with my first wife in East Harlem. Political scientist Ann Marie Buitrago said my book was "a hysterical anti-Communist diatribe ... [that] takes up where the government left off and pursues it with the same political objectives."

These people were undoubtedly the corps of Rosenberg groupies—people who might just as well have been members of the Flat Earth Society. But the response of Victor Navasky was more troublesome. I had known Navasky for years. When I entered Elisabeth Irwin High School in the seventh grade, he was president of the student body, six years ahead of me and a graduating senior. I had for years written regularly for *The Nation*, of which he was editor in chief and later publisher. Indeed, when I started work on the book, I consulted Victor frequently, and thanked him for his support in my acknowledgments. Hence my amazement when I picked up *The Nation* and found a front-page "review" in which he attacked the book in the crudest of political terms, arguing that it provided new ammunition for the Reagan presidency and its policies. Navasky complained that Joyce Milton and I assumed that the CP "was in fact a spy recruitment agency." He accused us of having an "obsession with the CP as a force of evil"—which, of course, it was. But worst of all, Navasky said the message of our book was that "two self-advertised lefties have found the Rosenbergs guilty: there was an internal Red menace all along; *it isn't so awful to have electrocuted two traitors or even to have abandoned those who defended them.*"

Others joined in. The Columbia University historian Eric Foner, with whom I had worked on the journal *Marxist Perspectives* and who ran in the same circles of mutual friends, offered his own review in the pages of the ultraleft-wing *Guardian*. Foner claimed that the book was poor scholarship and that we had committed the cardinal sin of giving credence to Tartakow, a professional FBI informer. But he gave away the game when he told what really bothered him: We were partisans of "liberal anticommunism," and our real "villain was the Communist Party."

Foner wrote that we treated the CP as "little more than a nest of spies and potential spies, men and women ... who 'put the dictates of Soviet policy' ahead of U.S. realities." He sought to establish, by quoting the new revisionist historians of American Communism, that the American CP actually "was Americanized almost in spite of itself."

What upset me was that Foner was not just another historian; he was the major Marxist historian in the United States, holding a coveted position at Columbia University, and soon to be president of both major American historical associations. To have him on the warpath against me was no small thing. Decades later, Foner would still be repeating his arguments against me on the Rosenberg case. Indeed, when the Meeropol brothers came out with a new edition of their own book, *We Are Your Sons: The Legacy of Ethel and Julius Rosenberg* (1986), Foner wrote the introduction, where he insisted that American Communists were part of a "complex and diverse" organization and that the CP was not the "nest of spies portrayed by the FBI." Moreover, he asserted that the Rosenbergs' prosecution grew out of a "determined effort to root out dissent," part of a broader pattern of "shattered careers and suppressed civil liberties." But if Joyce Milton and I had established anything, it was that the Rosenberg case resulted from a genuine effort to combat actual Soviet espionage. It was not the civil liberties of Julius Rosenberg that were being jeopardized, but the national interest.

To be fair, there were a few brave souls on the left who came to our book's defense. Both Katha Pollit and Maurice Isserman wrote small pieces supporting it in the pages of *The Nation*. Most important, however, was the lengthy defense of the book by Jim Weinstein, who took to the pages of his newspaper, *In These Times*, to defend it in the September 14–20, 1983, issue. Jim, of course, was the person whose doubts had started me out on a different path. But he was, and is still, an unreconstructed left-wing socialist, whose definition of socialism is a society based on the abolition of private property. So for him to back *The Rosenberg File* after the rest of the Left attacked it was an act of bravery for which I remain ever grateful. Given that Jim was privately critical of my 1979 *New Republic* article, his public response to the book indicated a welcome change. He wrote the following: "*The Rosenberg File* is a thoroughly and carefully researched book. Its conclusions flow from an overwhelming mass of evidence, carefully checked for corroboration wherever possible. It seems to me that any reader not encumbered with an ideological axe to grind would find Radosh's and Milton's conclusions convincing."

In a widely published column, David Rieff commented that the "fascinating" response to a book that did not "seem particularly controversial" to him stemmed from the fact that "the Rosenbergs are the American left's only true martyrs"; and martyrs, he wrote, "make things easy for those who remain." Rieff understood that if one found the Rosenbergs guilty, then one "must talk about Soviet espionage and not just about FBI iniquities." Perhaps for this reason, some brave souls who at first endorsed our effort suddenly retreated.

One of these, strangely, was the legendary journalist I. F. Stone. He had been a pro-Communist and later fellow-traveling figure throughout the 1930s and '40s, but by the late 1950s he had come to adopt an independent stance, challenging the official Communist Party line on scores of issues—at times from its right, at others from its left. After reading the article Sol Stern and I wrote about the case in the June 23, 1979, issue of the *New Republic,* he called up Holt, Rinehart and Winston, who had been identified as the future publisher of the book we were writing. Stone told our editor, Marian Wood, that he was more than excited about the prospect of this book. He wanted to help us in any way possible, he said. I recall Marian telling me, "Izzy can't wait for the book."

I soon traveled to Washington, D.C., and spent a day and a nice dinner with Stone and his wife at their beautiful home adjacent to the woods in Rock Creek Park. We had a conversation that ranged far and wide on scores of issues, from the Rosenberg case to the Soviet Union, to American politics and the nature of the American Left. Calling himself a simple *yeshiva bokher,* a Jewish scholar of the books who always sought the truth, Stone said that he believed apartheid South Africa was a freer society than the Soviet Union. He had, indeed, come a very long way from his fellow-traveling days. I reminded Stone that he had run an article on the case after reading the trial transcript, and had reached the conclusion that the couple was more than likely to have been guilty and that the trial proceedings were fair. He congratulated me on the fruits of my research, and reiterated that he would help the project in any way he could.

In fact, Joyce Milton and I decided to use as an epigram for the book the words from a column that Stone wrote in his newsletter on July 2, 1956:

> Who was telling the truth—the Rosenbergs or Greenglass? Who was telling the truth—Sobell or Elitcher? It will be a long time, if ever, before we know for certain. We may wake up one morning to learn that the Rosenbergs were guilty. We may wake up to learn that they were innocent. But I doubt whether we will ever find there was a deliberate frameup. Fanaticism had the same momentum on both sides.

Because of this comment and his friendship towards me after the 1979 article, I was taken aback to receive a phone call from Marian Wood shortly before the book was to be published. This time, her news was quite different: she had sent Stone an advance copy, and once again he had phoned her, informing her harshly that he did not endorse the book. If we did not remove the quotation, he said, he would sue us and Holt, Rinehart and Winston.

I wrote Izzy a tough but friendly letter in which I said, "To be asked by you now to delete a reference to your own views comes as astonishing and shocking. Coming from anyone else, I would consider it as a mandate for censorship." I never received any formal reply from Stone, but he phoned Wood to let her know that he had reconsidered, and would not oppose use of the quotation. Years later, he praised the book in an interview with journalist Andrew Patner, who authored a short account of Stone's life. But his immediate response—threatening to sue if we used his own words—indicates just how vulnerable even an independent leftist was on an article of faith such as the innocence of the Rosenbergs.

The Graduate Center forum committee at my own City University of New York contacted me about speaking on the Rosenbergs. I expected the same opportunity at my own home campus as Allen Weinstein had received when *Perjury* had appeared: he gave a long presentation about the Hiss case at an event chaired by Gertrude Himmelfarb, and then engaged in vigorous debate with the audience, which included his most prominent critics. To my amazement, however, the committee informed me that they would not sponsor a similar event, but instead would hold a debate between me and Walter and Miriam Schneir, the architects of the archetypical left-wing conspiracy theory on the case. I refused to accept that arrangement. The committee then presented the Schneirs by themselves, who came with handouts attacking *The Rosenberg File* at length.

Eventually, Joyce Milton, Sol Stern and I agreed to a major debate with the Schneirs and some of their supporters, to be held at New York's famous Town Hall on West Forty-third Street in October of 1983, a few months after the book's publication. Sponsored by the *New Republic* and *The Nation,* it quickly became "the hottest ticket in town," according to Ted Koppel of ABC's *Nightline.* The hall was filled to capacity, including a smattering of celebrities like my old roommate Marshall Brickman, and Woody Allen with his then companion, Mia Farrow. The debate was intense and lasted way over four hours. It was an event, one journalist accurately wrote, that "quickly degenerated into an inquisitional atmosphere with an ideological lynch mob leveling vicious character assassinations at Radosh and Milton," while another historian commented that it "resembled a medieval theological confrontation."

The Meeropols' counsel, Marshall Perlin, accused us of fabricating evidence with the cooperation of the FBI, to which I screamed in retort: "Left-wing McCarthyism!" The audience, three-quarters of whom were veterans of the Old Left—Communists and fellow travelers—got their anger out by constantly booing, screaming and insulting us at length during the question period. "How much did the FBI pay you?" yelled the noted "comedian" known as "Professor Irwin Corey." Standing up in his chair, Corey looked so agitated that some thought he was about to have a heart attack.

After the debate, exhausted from the somewhat volatile evening, I had another fifteen minutes of questions on *Nightline*, sitting next to Miriam Schneir, whose insults I had received the past few hours. *Nightline* devoted its entire hour to the debate, showed some excerpts, and had a long discussion of our book's importance. In addition, the new cable network CNN broadcast live through the night, and later, a documentary filmmaker bought their footage and edited a film about the event.

Soon after the appearance of *The Rosenberg File*, I attended the annual conference of the Organization of American Historians, held that year at a hotel in Los Angeles. I spotted my old acquaintance Paul Buhle in the hotel lobby, and walked over to say hello. When he saw me, he quickly began walking away, but I managed to catch up. He paused, looked at me and said, "You really are a running dog of imperialism, aren't you?" Then he mixed his metaphor by clicking his heels and walking away. Later that evening, returning from a long evening with friends, I was heading to the hotel elevator near midnight. The lobby was virtually empty, and once again, Buhle appeared coming in the front door. This time he walked up to me and said, "How are you? I didn't want to talk with you when everyone would see me, but there's nobody here now." It was my turn to walk away.

I also received my share of middle-of-the-night, threatening phone calls, many of them—as one would expect—anonymous. One person who called, though, was an old Camp Woodland friend, who coincidentally had recently joined DSOC. She was Joni Rabinowitz, daughter of the radical lawyer Victor Rabinowitz, who had been one of the first people Julius Rosenberg approached to be his counsel before settling on Emanuel Bloch. I had interviewed Rabinowitz and quoted him in the introduction, without giving his name. I related how he

> began our conversation by slamming his fist on his desk and bellowing: "Of course they were guilty. But you can't quote me. My public position is that the Rosenbergs were innocent." And he elaborated: "What's wrong with what they did? If I were in their place, I would have done the same thing.... It was the respon-

sibility of a good Communist to do whatever he could to help the Red Army gain victory." Then ... he reiterated, "Don't think I'm so dumb that I don't believe the Rosenbergs weren't engaged in espionage."

I did not name Rabinowitz in the book because he told me in advance that he would deny the statement, and that I could not quote him by name. Now, Joni was calling me from Pittsburgh and screaming on the phone: "I just want you to know that you are a traitor! Your book is a vile lie and you shouldn't have written it." "Have you read it?" I asked her. "Of course not," she replied. "I'm not going to honor you by wasting my time seeing what you have said. You had a responsibility not to write that book and you did it anyway. I'm only sorry that I now belong to the same organization you do. You're nothing but a damned bastard as far as I'm concerned." At least she was paying for the long-distance call.

One other episode related to the book revealed the tremendous power of the Left. When it came time to sell the book to paperback, a small auction, as it is called in the trade, took place. The final competition came down to two firms, Penguin and Vintage Books, the paper outlet of Random House. Penguin promised to leave it in print for a very lengthy period and sell it to the college market. But Vintage was known for doing a better job of publicity and being able to sell as well to the mass market, not just the college trade. They made a good offer, and Joyce and I accepted it.

We wrote a new introduction for the paper edition, and the galleys were quickly readied. The book included quotations from most of the rave reviews. With the attention it had received already, we expected a new round of publicity and hearty sales. So it was a great shock to receive a letter from the new editor in chief of Vintage Books informing us that although the book was already printed and ready for distribution, Vintage would cancel publication and not release it. The editor explained that she had received a letter from the American historian Richard Drinnon, who was then teaching at Bucknell University. Drinnon told her that our book was a historical fraud based on spurious scholarship. That such a distinguished, tenured faculty member could make these charges, she said, was enough for her to cancel publication.

Marian Wood, the original editor at Holt, quickly got on the phone after consulting with Holt's lawyers. She pointed out that Vintage had asked for and acquired the book, and had signed a contract to publish it. For them to rescind publication because of a smear by one radical academic was illegal. That call to Vintage was sufficient to get them to go ahead with publication. But Vintage did almost no advertising for the book, and no publicity; they did not arrange or try to receive any radio or TV interviews, nor would there be another book tour. They may have been legally forced to publish our book, as required by contract, but they were not obligated to do anything to make people aware of its existence.

I write these concluding words on the Rosenberg episode in the early part of the twenty-first century. One would think that by now, with so much time having passed, the case would no longer be controversial. In one sense, the thesis we advanced in the Rosenberg case has stood the test of time. As we wrote in the new Yale University Press edition of *The Rosenberg File* (1997), the release of the Venona files in 1995 proved conclusively that Julius Rosenberg committed espionage against the United States on behalf of the Soviet Union. With these files, and with the public admission of Alexsandr Feklisov, the Rosenbergs' control in the United States, about how he handled and recruited Julius Rosenberg, all doubts were laid to rest.

In an extremely important article that appeared in the *New York Review of Books* on May 11, 2000, Thomas Powers pointed out that recent documents from the former Soviet Union have "illuminated and sometimes even definitely settled many controversies about the guilt or innocence of people accused during the 1950s of having spied for the Soviet Union." Joe McCarthy's rough-and-tumble methods, he noted, had led many liberals "to deny overheated right-wing charges of subversion with counterclaims that the 'Red Menace' was all being trumped up by the FBI." Powers went on to explain:

> Soviet spies were of the left generally, they supported liberal
> causes, they defended the Soviet Union in all circumstances, they
> were often secret members of the Communist Party, they were
> uniformly suspicious of American initiatives throughout the
> world, they could be contemptuous of American democracy, soci-
> ety and culture, and above all, their offenses were often mini-
> mized or explained away by apologists who felt that no man
> should be called traitor who did what he did for the cause of
> humanity.

The truth, as Powers wrote, is that the Soviet Union "recruited
[spies] from the ranks of the left ... ran them to steal secrets,
and when they got caught at it they went to ground and waited
for a better day." He might have well added, as my own experience shows, that those who told the truth became the victims
of an unprecedented smear attack, one that sought to rescue
the myth by blaming the messengers who brought bad news
about it.

So, in 2001, it is almost a battle won. Still, a few holdouts
always will exist. My friends and colleagues Harvey Klehr and
John E. Haynes—authors of classic studies of American communism and the Venona papers—revealed in the April 10, 2000,
issue of the *Weekly Standard* that the venerable and highly
regarded *American National Biography*, the standard reference
work for the public on major figures in our past, commissioned
the Communist historian Norman Markowitz to write the cur-
rent entry on the Rosenberg case. His entry proclaims that only
"conservative writers" and "anti-Communist or Cold War liberals" had an "unquestioning belief in the Rosenbergs' guilt," while
upholding their innocence was "the most significant expression
of resistance to the spread of the domestic Cold War by ... radicals and anti–Cold War liberals." Hence, as Klehr and Haynes
write, the *American National Biography*'s editors have allowed a
"distortion of historical fact to be palmed off on many thousands
of unsuspecting students for decades to come."

The problem is one of the American academy, which for
some reason remains the repository of the unreconstructed remnants of the Old and New Left, secure in their ability to continue
to advance their old myths as if the world around them had not

changed. For these people, it is still the 1950s, the Soviet Union holds out the beacon of hope and socialism, and the United States stands with the forces of fascism and war. As for me, the experience I had writing, researching and watching the reaction to *The Rosenberg File* helped to push me towards a fundamental reconsideration of once firmly held beliefs.

Although I didn't fully realize it at the time, the reaction to *The Rosenberg File* made me finally move on to consider the ultimate heresy: perhaps the Left was wrong not just about the Rosenberg case, but about most everything else. Perhaps, I thought—but quickly buried the heresy—the entire socialist project was wrong. As events of the 1980s began to unfold, my journey to America was about to reach its final leg.

Adventures in Sandinistaland

I TRIED HARD TO SWALLOW THE DOUBTS ABOUT THE LEFT I WAS beginning to harbor as a result of my encounter with the unquiet ghosts of Julius and Ethel Rosenberg, but that experience stuck in my craw. Although I didn't want to be excommunicated from the church of the Left where I had worshipped all of my life, I had in fact started to question the whole project of the Left. Soon I would learn what so many in similar circumstances had seen before me: that there is a straight line leading from doubt to apostasy.

For the time being, however, I tried to rekindle my faith by involvement in the civil war in El Salvador. Not without a certain relief, the Left saw another Vietnam in our hemispheric backyard and confidently predicted that within a few years, American ground troops would be involved in another "quagmire" closer to home. Along with some of my old friends, I worked on a book about the crisis, *El Salvador: Central America in the New Cold War*. Published in 1981 by the venerable left-wing publisher Grove Press, the book was meant to be a reader for a new anti-interventionist movement.

I attended the requisite number of street demonstrations and organized a folk music benefit concert on behalf of the Salvadoran guerrillas' mass front group, the Revolutionary Democratic Front, usually referred to as the FDR. On a simple level, we repeated ad infinitum the argument that rather than being a pro-Soviet revolutionary group, the FDR was a multi-tendency reformist movement dominated by Social Democrats and Christian Democrats. The rebellion, we asserted, was an indigenous protest against a repressive government that bolstered the power of old-style, landowning oligarchs, resisted true land reform, and was forcing a forbidden civilian opposition into the posture of armed struggle.

These claims were offered with all the old passion of the 1960s; but as time went on, their fallacy became difficult to deny. We spoke about the "popular support" for the FDR and its military wing, which was preparing for what they called "the Final Offensive." But the threat of a last apocalyptic push backfired when poor and working-class areas in the small nation failed to rise in defense of their would-be revolutionary saviors. As the United States government backed the reformist Salvadoran president Jose Napoleon Duarte, himself once a political exile from military dictatorship, the guerrillas falsely portrayed him as a tool of the extreme right wing and the military, rather than admitting that he presented a legitimate alternative to the "death squads" of the extreme Right and of the revolutionary Left.

While the Salvadoran revolutionaries' assault on Duarte seemed increasingly filled with ambiguity, a different situation had developed in Nicaragua, where the Sandinista Front for National Liberation (FSLN) had won an armed conflict with the forces of dictator Anastasio Somoza. The Sandinista "triumph" in 1979 was heralded by the international Left as a giant step in the direction of socialism and freedom. Like Castro in 1959, the Sandinistas pledged to create a broad, humane new democratic government, one that included representation from all elements of the old democratic opposition to the Somoza dictatorship, and that would not be totalitarian.

Within a very few months, however, the true character of the new regime became apparent. Those with arms—the Sandinista military—set the agenda, and the representation of civilians in the governing junta was proved to be short lived. Power was concentrated in the hands of twelve different revolutionary *commandantes,* each from a different pre-takeover revolutionary group, and each with his own private army, supporter groups, and assorted sycophants. Eventually, the top position would go to Commandante Daniel Ortega and his brother Humberto, who assumed control of the armed forces.

Initially I was delighted that Mike Harrington offered his, and DSOC's, backing to this revolution. Mike became the American representative to the Socialist International's so-called "Committee to Defend the Nicaraguan Revolution." Playing on the old "domino theory" from the war in Southeast Asia—when U.S. officials argued that if Vietnam was allowed to fall to the Communists, this would knock down other non-Communist nations in the region—Harrington called Sandinista Nicaragua "the good domino." He painted the FSLN as a democratic alternative to an old-style dictatorship of the Right or the Left, and a model for a future Central America that would be independent of U.S. control and free to determine its own political destiny. Harrington visited Managua for a three-day stay. After meeting privately with the revolutionary directorate, he was, as he wrote, "deeply moved by the sincerity and passion of those with whom I talked." He went on to argue that whatever excesses the *commandantes* had committed could be traced to the policy of the United States, which refused to grant them aid or political support. He thought the Sandinista revolution was essentially "democratic and pluralist" by nature, but that the American response might push it to left-wing extremism. It was what might be called the Flip Wilson effect: The devil made me do it.

Ortega and company knew what to say, and it was easy to seduce an American democratic socialist who was hoping that this time around, revolution would yield something different from the horrors it had always produced before. Mike Harrington knew that reactionary private-sector interests, as he defined them, were already describing the Sandinista leaders as "Stalinist," yet he was not about to follow suit. I too hoped that what was taking place in Nicaragua was something different, a truly human, democratic radicalism that would allow multiparty rule and a soft welfare state with a thriving private economy—something, in other words, that would rescue the Left from itself. Yet I couldn't ignore evidence that this was not the case. I insisted, with others on the left, that a brutal war against the Sandinistas was being waged by the U.S.-backed *contras,* the anti-Sandinista guerrilla fighters supported by the Reagan administration, who adopted the name from the term scornfully used against them, "counterrevolutionary."

In 1981, my friend Louis Menashe and I contributed an op-ed piece to the *New York Times*, in which we argued that revolution was not being "exported" to the region, that its causes were entirely indigenous, and that a leftist victory would result in a mixed economy and a democratic government that would reject the revolutionary path. But my work on the Rosenberg case and the reaction to it had taught me that the truth may be troubling and the Left may be wrong. They might be wrong about the Sandinistas, too. I was determined to travel to Nicaragua and judge the situation for myself. I convinced the editors of the *New Republic,* who were also growing skeptical about the Sandinista agenda, to send me there in 1983 to observe the revolution.

The Inter-Continental in Managua, virtually the only intact hotel in the country since the Somoza-era earthquake, was humming with activity. Journalists from all over the world, international celebrities, foreign revolutionaries and revolutionary groupies swarmed into the city center. I began by meeting and spending time with Stephen Kinzer, then the *New York Times* correspondent for Central America. Kinzer was sharp and friendly, and all the freelancers, fresh off the plane, gravitated to him, especially the hordes of women who hoped that writing about Nicaragua would give their careers a jump start. He also had access to an air-conditioned car. Once, I took a jeep ride with the assistant minister of agriculture to cover a ceremony for the dispensing of some land deeds, a trip in which the temperature in the closed-in vehicle was well over one hundred degrees, leaving me drenched in sweat and dizzy. Kinzer was at the ceremony. He smiled at me and said, "I bet you wished you drove out with me in my air-conditioned car." I was thankful beyond measure when he offered to take me back to Managua at day's end.

One afternoon, sitting in the Inter-Continental lobby to see who would turn up, I spotted a sultry-looking woman engaged in heated dialogue with a man I didn't recognize. I realized that the mysterious beauty was Bianca Jagger. Born into an upper-class Nicaraguan family, the famous model and ex-wife of Mick Jagger was now beginning her transformation from a denizen of Studio 54 to supporter of Third World revolutions, including the one in her own native land. Bianca, it turned out, was traveling with someone I knew vaguely from the New York folk scene, an itinerant journalist and folk singer who was a top-notch Bob Dylan imitator, and who had decided to become her informal political advisor. I sat down next to them and started up a conversation. I found Bianca to be accessible and friendly, and willing to engage in frank dialogue about the revolution's strengths and weaknesses. She told me, for example, that the Sandinistas had unfairly confiscated her brother's home, and that she tried to argue with them that this kind of behavior towards their own supporters was foolhardy.

Over the following days, I saw Bianca many times, and I took up her offer to interview her at length about her life, her views and her politics. She wanted to be taken seriously. "I have this unjust reputation of being a Studio 54 dilettante," she said, "and it's not correct. Everyone compares me to Jane Fonda, and that's not right either." She did her best to convince me that she simply wanted to help her native land gain its freedom, and that despite their faults, the Sandinistas were serious and on the right path. Then we began to talk about the *commandantes,* and she blurted out, "Tomas Borge, I think, is the best."

This statement struck me as bizarre, given that most observers considered the head of State Security as the most hard-line and repressive of all the Sandinista leaders. But then I began to see why she had this opinion. A few nights a week, Borge would appear at the Inter-Continental, go up to her suite, and not descend until sometime near morning. The hotel lobby would be filled with his personal security force, armed with submachine guns, their jeeps parked outside the main entrance. A forlorn *Newsweek* correspondent who was also courting Bianca would wait in the bar until Borge left, in the hopes that she would be able to squeeze him in. Bianca also tended to wear loose, transparent clothing. Once, the photographer from the *New Orleans Times-Picayune* came running through the lobby, having just emerged from the elevator, screaming, "I just saw Bianca Jagger's tits! I saw her tits!" (I have to confess that the photographer's observation was not unusual. As I interviewed Bianca in her hotel suite, she would slowly unbutton her blouse to reveal her bosom, and then slowly rebutton it.) Such was the journalistic world in Managua, 1983.

My article appeared in a special issue of the *New Republic* devoted to Central America, published on October 24, 1983. I began by saying that both extreme views of the revolution were wrong: that of the conservative movement, which saw it as a stolen revolution already turned Stalinist; and that of the Left, which saw it as a popular nationalist revolution similar to our own. I concluded, after a month in the country, that the Sandinista rule was not totalitarian, but its leaders had totalitarian ambitions and the country was sadly moving in that direction. Quoting a high source in the United States Embassy, I agreed that political space was constricting, and that the civil war worked to the Sandinistas' advantage, permitting them to blame their already serious internal problems on the United States. I opposed the measures used by the Reagan administration to restore democracy in Nicaragua: "Subsidizing the *contras'* war and economic strangulation so far have worked to bolster support for the Sandinistas."

I thought I was being balanced, but my criticism of the Sandinistas was not taken kindly by the friends I still had on the political left after the fracas over the Rosenberg case. Any criticism of the *commandantes,* I kept hearing, gave aid and comfort to the enemy—in this case, the United States. At this time, for instance, Paul Berman, later a friendly critic of the Sandinistas, was writing regularly in his *Village Voice* column that the only correct position was to focus on the human rights abuses of the *contras* and on the Reagan administration's support of them. The problem with this view was that while the *contras* were indeed guilty of abusing human rights, so were the Sandinistas; and neither Berman nor anyone else in the self-proclaimed "responsible" Left wanted to scrutinize them.

Over the next year or so, it became clearer to me that in fact, the various rebel groups comprising the Sandinista Front were ultrarevolutionary Marxist-Leninists, and that their inspiration and support came from the Soviet Union and Fidel Castro's Cuba rather than from the U.S. Declaration of Independence. Moreover, a serious movement for reform of *contra* human rights abuses arose, as the armed opponents of the Sandinista government slowly became an authentic indigenous opposition, rather than the fascist bandits of leftist fantasy. The real character of the revolution was becoming clear. After being served up as an exotic hors d'oeuvre at radical-chic parties in Hollywood and elsewhere during his trip to the United States, Daniel Ortega proclaimed a state of emergency back home, suspending all civil liberties and political rights, including those to "seek, receive and spread information and ideas." The Sandinista regime attacked the Miskito Indians on the Caribbean Coast and began to use Soviet attack helicopters against the *contras*.

It was clear to me that the Sandinistas' new emergency decrees were not aimed at guerrilla opponents, but at domestic dissidents, including labor militants who opposed the harsh antilabor measures of the revolutionary government. Those who opposed wage cuts, for example, were accused of economic sabotage and thrown into prison. Bianca Jagger's friend, State Security Minister Borge, said that his government was pledged to use "coercion by the state" against those in opposition, to establish new people's courts and, if necessary, to assassinate major opposition figures.

In the *New York Times* I wrote that while I still opposed the *contras*, I also opposed cheerleading for the Sandinistas. This, of course, inflamed the Left. At one debate held at Hunter College, critics of U.S. Central American policy refused to let me speak. Privately, some of my friends said I might be right, but, as one of them put it, "Your timing is wrong. The Sandinistas are under attack, and we have to support them."

Still, the issue of the *contras* was a sticking point for me. When Penn Kemble, later deputy director of the United States Information Agency during the Clinton administration but then an active leader of the Social Democrats USA (the group from which Mike Harrington had split), defended an active pro-*contra* policy in the pages of *Commentary*, I wrote a lengthy rebuttal, saying that such a policy was both immoral and counterproductive.

Kemble's answer was serious and tough-minded, and as I read it fifteen years later, I find it thoroughly convincing. He pointed to solid evidence, of which much more has been unearthed since the end of the 1980s, about how U.S. efforts to befriend the new Sandinista government were totally rejected, finally forcing the Carter administration to cut off aid to Nicaragua in January 1981. Kemble asked me something I could not answer: "In the light of this history, how can it still be argued that it is the *contras* who are making Communists out of the Sandinistas?" Indeed, Kemble saw evidence proving that the slide towards totalitarianism in Nicaragua was seriously slowed by the guerrillas' military fight. And he argued that in reality the *contras* were a movement in transition from a proxy military force to a serious rallying point for disaffected peasants.

To my surprise, Kemble not only sent me this letter, but called me up. "You should go to Nicaragua to see the *contra* camps," he suggested. "You should observe and talk with them. You'll see that they're peasants who want freedom, and not Somocistas from the old right-wing elites of the country." I mulled over his proposal, and said that if he could arrange a trip, I would go with an open mind. Within a few weeks, Kemble had obtained plane tickets for me and told me to purchase protective clothing that would blend in with the surroundings—essentially camouflage. Outside of old Army-Navy stores, the only place that sold such items was the ritzy new Banana Republic store, which had just opened in my neighborhood. I purchased the required green T-shirts, netting, and a good sun hat; and then, feeling somewhat foolish, I awaited my trip.

A week before I was scheduled to leave, I got a phone call from Sidney Blumenthal, then a national desk reporter at the *Washington Post* and a man I had known slightly from his days at the socialist publication *In These Times*. He had heard through the grapevine that I was scheduled to travel to Nicaragua. Blumenthal said nothing about any plan to write a story. Posing as a "friend" rather than a journalist, he warned me about Kemble and his associates: While they pretended to be social democrats, he said, "they're tied in to the extreme right wing. You should be cautious about having anything to do with them."

I told him that I disagreed with Kemble's support of the *contras*, but I had no reason not to observe their base and see for myself. "Are you sure that you're going?" Blumenthal asked. "I'd better be!" I quipped. "I have a plane ticket, and shirts and a hat that I just bought at Banana Republic."

A day later, when I was on vacation in Cape Cod, I received a phone call from a friend in Washington, D.C. "Did you see today's *Washington Post* yet?" he asked. "Blumenthal has a whole news report about you and your impending trip to the *contra* camp." When I got the article a few days later I was shocked to see the headline: "Professor to Visit Contras: Buys Clothes at Banana Republic." The rest of the article asserted that while bona fide journalists were being kept from reporting on the *contras*, I was somehow going to their forbidden sites, courtesy of the right wing. The article also reported in detail how I prepared for the journey by shopping at the tony clothing store. It was a typical slander by a man who would become the Roy Cohn of the Clinton administration a few years later.

Then Kemble called to inform me that the trip had been called off. Fearing that I had purposely leaked the story to Blumenthal in order to make the *contras* appear foolish, the Central Intelligence Agency, which was monitoring and arranging the trips by journalists to see the *contras*, insisted that I could no longer be trusted to travel there.

I was swayed by Kemble's pointed argument, yet tried to straddle the issue by criticizing both the *contras* and the Sandinistas. It was not a posture I could maintain for long, especially as word continued to spread of increasing Sandinista abuse of human rights.

Through Bob Leiken, who had edited a collection on Central America I had reviewed for the *New York Times Book Review,* and who subsequently became my good friend, I learned about a young human rights activist named Nina Shea, executive director of a small Catholic human rights group called the Puebla Institute. Shea, he said, was looking for someone to accompany her on a trip through Central America to interview Nicaraguan refugees and prepare a report on Sandinista human rights violations. I went to a panel on which Shea was speaking in New York, and after introducing myself to her, told her that I wanted to apply to be part of the Puebla mission she was planning.

Early in 1987, we visited refugee camps set up by the U.N. High Commission on Refugees in both Costa Rica and Honduras. It was a grueling and moving experience. Thousands of peasants were living on dry, desolate land, in makeshift shacks and tents in sweltering heat. Sanitary conditions were deplorable. The smell of raw sewage was everywhere; the stink of the latrines hung heavily in the fetid air. As we talked with the inhabitants, day after day, we heard countless stories of how these people had their hopes and dreams shattered by the Sandinistas. One man, who described himself as a former militant of the revolution, walked for days across the country to escape through the Costa Rican border.

I flashed back to my trip to Cuba ten years earlier and to the proscribed homosexuals and victims of "socialist lobotomies" I had seen there. They were not counterrevolutionaries or "worms," as Castro called them, but ordinary people who suffered the revolution's wrath. Likewise, the people Nina Shea and I were interviewing were not *contras,* but rather simple peasants who found their land and livelihoods taken from them by revolutionaries who had postured as their saviors, only to become their masters. As I heard about the kind of repression and violence they faced daily in their homeland, I realized that all during the decades of Somoza rule, Nicaragua never had refugees. I was probably someone waiting for a conversion experience; now it had arrived. I left these refugees confirmed that Sandinista power in Nicaragua had to be ended.

During our press conference at the end of January 1987, when we had returned to New York, we reported on our main finding: accounts by many refugees of indiscriminate bombing on civilian areas by Sandinista military forces. We also related testimony about shooting attacks by armed forces on civilians, as well as the destruction of houses, schools and personal property. Specifically, we told of an attack that took place on December 9,

1986, in Punta Gorda, a town on the Atlantic Coast, in which the army used MI Hind-24 Soviet attack helicopters and two planes to bomb the area. Except for the *Washington Times,* the relatively new conservative paper in the nation's capital, and the *New York Post,* our news conference was blacked out. We stressed that the Sandinistas' tactics—killing citizens and "pacifying" their farms and villages lest they become havens for the *contras*—were the same kind of resettlement policy that the Left accused the United States of using in Vietnam. The difference was that now the Left was completely silent.

It was not until the following May that front-page reports by William Branigan in the *Washington Post* and James LeMoyne in the *New York Times* documented much of what we had previously uncovered and published in *Fleeing Their Homeland,* the Puebla Institute's report of our visit. These reports confirmed the San-dinista record of imprisonment and torture of dissenters, attacks on the civilian population, and aerial bombing.

On May 20, 1987, I sent a letter to journalist Paul Berman, who had been an outspoken critic of *contra* human rights abuses. "The time has come," I wrote, "when someone like yourself can no longer remain silent. The evidence is rather incontrovertible: the Sandinistas are no better than their right-wing counterparts." I scolded Berman for ignoring a *New Republic* article I had writ-ten on the Sandinistas' bombing of civilians, and implicitly cred-iting the propaganda of the Sandinista ambassador to the United Nations, Nora Astorga, who denounced our reports as lies. "Don't people like yourself, who are in the forefront of oppos-ing U.S. foreign policy, have the responsibility to condemn the Sandinistas?"

I wrote a similar letter to my old Elisabeth Irwin High School classmate Mary Travers (of Peter, Paul and Mary), who had appeared in Nicaragua as a guest of Ortega and company. I sent her my *New Republic* article and a long review I had written of several pro-Sandinista books. I asked her whether she thought it was right that only the Reagan administration, which I knew she detested, was left to criticize the documented abuse of human rights carried on by the Sandinistas. "The least you could do," I wrote, "is no longer give parties for the Sandinista leaders, or go to the country and appear solely as their guests.... Why don't you ask to go to interview the opposition and the political prisoners in Nicaragua?"

Mary never replied. Berman did not write back, although I did speak to him on the phone, when he declared that as far as he was concerned, "the only issue is the *contras*." In a nutshell, this was the position of most of the Left, whose anti-Americanism, its most precious heirloom from the Vietnam War, had to be preserved at all costs. Whatever the sins of the Sandinistas, since the U.S. was opposing them, they had to be supported. Those of us who pointed to what the Sandinista power meant for regular Nicaraguans, including working-class Nicaraguans active in trade unions, were completely ignored. Eventually, Paul Berman would become something of a critic of the Sandinistas, and would use this as proof of how he exemplified a truly independent and critical left wing. But his tepid criticism would be too little and too late, coming after it could do any good.

I soon received a phone call from Irving Howe, who let me know that as a member of the editorial board of *Dissent,* as well as an active member of Harrington's DSOC, I was causing his group problems by my continuing public criticism of the Sandinistas. Howe asked that I come to his apartment one evening, where he said he would gather some of the most important *Dissent* editors and democratic socialist activists to discuss my position.

If anyone should have been skeptical of the Sandinistas, it was Irving Howe. He had been a leader of the anti-Stalinist Left for decades, and his good friend and Latin American counterpart, the critic and poet Octavio Paz, had written widely against the Sandinistas, pointing out that they were a sectarian, pro-Soviet group and a danger to the people of Latin America. But Howe was not about to join in his criticism. As I entered his apartment in New York City's East 80s off Fifth Avenue, I found a relatively small group, including Debbie Meier and other editors and activists. Howe suggested that I listen first to what they had to

say. They all spoke in turn. Meier was the most angry and vocif-
erous. "You may be right about what you say about the Sandinistas," she stated, "but while they are under attack by the
American empire, we have a responsibility to extend our solidarity to them." The time, in other words, was never right. Howe
himself argued that the Sandinistas were "something new," not
a traditional Marxist-Leninist group, but perhaps a "third force"
alternative to both right-wing authoritarianism and Stalinism.
What really upset me, however, was Howe's remark at the end:
"We have agreed," he said, "that you cannot write on Nicaragua
in the pages of *Dissent*. You may write on anything else, but not
on this topic." So, the heralded democratic socialist quarterly
was banning me from its pages. My dissent was obviously too
much for *Dissent* to bear.

Countering Howe, I pulled out what I thought was my trump
card. A leading Nicaraguan trade unionist, a man who led the
Social Democrats in that country, had written a public "May Day
letter" to workers in Nicaragua sharply criticizing the *commandantes* for their violation of human rights and suppression of
strikes and trade union activity. Because the letter had been
banned in Nicaragua by the Sandinistas, I suggested that Howe
at least reprint it as "A Message from a Nicaraguan Dissident."
I told him, "You have done the same numerous times for brave
Soviet dissidents, at a time when they had no other voice. It was
in your pages that I first heard about the trial in Russia of some
of the first writers suppressed in the Brezhnev era." Howe took
the man's statement from me to see who had distributed it in
this country. The logo indicated it was an effort of the AFL-CIO's
American Institute for Free Labor Development (AIFLD), which
had set up efforts to promote democratic unionism in the Third
World, centering on Latin and Central America. Howe grimaced
and said, "As far as I'm concerned, this man is probably a CIA
agent, and we won't print his statement."

Four years after I had gone to Nicaragua to witness the revolution, I returned for a short trip and wrote "Nicaragua Revisited:
The Sandinistas' Growing Totalitarianism," which appeared in
the *New Republic* in August 1987. I found, much as many oth-

ers who had broken with the regime were claiming, that there were now "few signs of pluralism, and government repression has become fierce and pervasive." I found evidence of the type of repression one heard about regularly in the region's authoritarian right-wing and military-dominated governments. But when the Sandinistas engaged in similar practices, the voices of the American opponents of U.S. policy were silent. They may have given great publicity to the famous Mothers' Movement in Argentina, when heroic mothers of the "disappeared" picketed regularly in front of government offices, protesting the arrest, torture and murder of their loved ones by the Argentinian military junta in the 1980s. But when Nicaraguan mothers took a leaf from their book and formed the January 3 Movement of Mothers of Political Prisoners, and State Security agents immediately threatened them with imprisonment, it was virtually ignored in the United States.

In November of 1987, I returned to Nicaragua on two more trips. The first was a short visit sponsored by the United States Information Agency, in which David Horowitz, Peter Collier and I spoke with Managua's "civic resistance" about how to use protest to promote democracy. There, we once again came across Paul Berman, who was in the country to write for various magazines. Berman got into a fight with David Horowitz and Peter Collier at a luncheon, when they tried to bait him into accompanying them to the long-awaited reopening of Violeta Chamorro's paper, *La Prensa,* which had been shut down by the Sandinista censors. They told him this was a triumph for openness, which ought to be supported; but Berman—like Irving Howe, still seeking a "third force"—had an appointment scheduled with a pro-Sandinista, self-proclaimed Christian Democrat, which he said was more important.

The celebration at *La Prensa* was jubilant, a moment signaling clearly that the Sandinistas' days were numbered. The paper printed a banner headline, "Triumph of the People," alluding to victory over the censors, but also meant as a challenge to the Sandinistas, who had used that very slogan for their own day of victory when they marched into Managua after the revolution in

1979. The irony was not lost on the public, which grabbed up every available copy of *La Prensa*.

A few weeks later, I traveled again to Central America, this time as part of an eight-person delegation led by Mayor Ed Koch of New York. Koch, who as a congressman had worked hard to cut off aid to Somoza, and who had welcomed Daniel Ortega to New York after his victory, was particularly concerned with the ongoing conflict in Central America and more than a bit cha-grined that he, like other liberals, had been conned by the sweet talk of Ortega, only to find that he was a low-rent version of Fidel Castro. As a consequence, Koch took the daring step of trying to intervene publicly in the Central American debate, which resulted in scores of major editorials denouncing him for trying to forge a New York City foreign policy.

A good politician, Koch was careful to include two obvious leftists in his delegation: Isaura Santiago-Santiago, a Hispanic Marxist who was president of Hostos Community College, the largely Puerto Rican institution that was part of New York's City University; and Harriet Richardson Michel, then president of the New York Urban League. The other six in the group included Charles Hughes, an African-American trade union leader; R. Peter Straus, radio magnate and former Voice of America chief; Richard Ravitch, CEO of the Bowery Savings Bank and former head of the New York Transit Authority; Mario Paredes, director of the North East Hispanic Catholic Center; and Ted Sorenson, the former special counsel to President John F. Kennedy. I was there due to the urging of my good friend the late Eric Brein-del, then editorial page editor of the *New York Post*, who stren-uously lobbied Koch to include me.

To prepare for the trip, we met privately with Oscar Arias, the president of Costa Rica, who was then proposing his much-heralded peace plan for Central America, for which he would later win the Nobel Peace Prize. At Gracie Mansion in New York, Mayor Koch arranged a long working dinner and reception, where we had a chance to talk at length with Arias about his hopes for the region. It was clear that although he had critics on both his left and his right, Arias was strongly opposed to the San-dinistas, with their clear hostility to political democracy. As he told us, "we may soon see the Communist government of Nicaragua using force against workers, students, peasants and intellectuals." Arias was ecstatic about the Koch mission; he gave it his blessings, and hoped that the mayor's journey would promote regional reconciliation and increase the chances for peace.

A day or so after the meeting with President Arias, the regularly scheduled *Dissent* editorial board meeting took place, as usual, at Debbie Meier's brownstone. Irving Howe was clearly angry, and couldn't hold his tongue. He began by lashing out at me for going on the Koch trip, and said that if I had any integrity, I would immediately resign from the appointment and denounce the mission. On the other hand, like other liberals, Howe had only praise for the announced terms of the Arias peace plan, on which he and others pinned their hopes for an end to the region's warfare. I replied that I had just come from a meeting with Arias himself, who was fully backing Koch's venture. Howe once again blasted the *contras,* calling them terrorists and thugs who deserved only scorn. He had little, if anything, negative to say about the Sandinistas. I recall that my friend Sol Stern, who was sitting in on the meeting, pointed out that the PLO were avowed terrorists, yet many of the *Dissent* editors favored meeting with them and supported their grievances.

The mission took us throughout the region, to Honduras, El Salvador, Guatemala, Costa Rica and, of course, Nicaragua, where we spent most of our time. Mayor Koch released a statement of the mission's goals upon our arrival in Managua on November 5, stressing our desire to help reach the goals of "reconciliation, amnesty, democratization, a negotiated ceasefire, and an end to the cross-border supplying of irregular forces." We urged a halt to external support of irregular military forces, called for economic aid and refugee relief, and recommended moving away from extremes and towards "the democratic center."

The statement was ambiguous, of course, and did little to ease growing tensions within our group of eight. The most visible sign of this occurred at a giant rally the Sandinistas held in Managua, when Ortega made his much-touted change in strategy. For months, the Sandinistas had argued that they would not negotiate with the *contras,* who were gaining in strength; they would only negotiate directly with the United States, which Ortega called the "puppet-masters." But at the rally, he abruptly changed course, announcing that he would now negotiate indirectly with the hated *contras,* through the good offices of the archbishop of Managua. As Ortega spoke his words of concession, Commandate Bayardo Arce, head of the party apparatus, visibly grimaced. At the same time, however, Ortega gave notice that his junta would continue to play hardball with the domestic civic opposition, and would use the state-sponsored goons, whom they called *turbas divinas* or "divine mobs," to crack heads if they protested too much.

Our delegation noticed immediately upon arriving that eight seats had been put on stage for us, directly behind President Ortega, who was going to introduce us during his speech. Koch told us he intended to inform the Sandinistas that our delegation was not there to give its support to Daniel Ortega or to endorse the party's agenda, but rather to speak in favor of democratization and peace. At that point, the radical women on the delegation, Isaura Santiago-Santiago and Harriet Richardson Michel, announced that they were not going to insult the Sandinistas like that, but would instead offer their support. Koch, by now madder than I had ever seen him, ordered them not to dare go onto the stage with such an action in mind. Smoldering, the two retreated, and later screamed at me that I was responsible, especially since earlier on the trip I had openly challenged a Sandinista spokesman about the movement's agenda. As it turned out, the rally had all the trappings of an orchestrated, fascist-style event. Indeed, Koch aroused the ire of many when he remarked at a press conference that the event, with its floodlights and great, shouting throngs, reminded him most of the Nazi Nuremberg rally.

Although we had met with the leaders of all the nations we visited—in El Salvador we met with Jose Napoleon Duarte at the president's palace, and in Costa Rica, with Arias—we had not yet had a meeting with Ortega. Finally, on the last night of our stay, Ortega informed our delegation that he would speak with us. The meeting was scheduled for 11 P.M. in a middle-class suburb of Managua. We arrived at the appointed time and waited and waited. Then, close to 3 A.M., when we were about to give up and retreat to our hotel rooms, Ortega phoned to say that the meeting was on. It was a common trick employed by totalitarians of the Left in Third World countries: keep visitors waiting until the last moment to impress them by how busy the leaders are, and how much more important than those who idle away hours just to see them.

We each got the chance to address a question to the first *commandante*. When it came my turn, I asked if the Sandinistas favored a "revolution without frontiers." Ortega looked at me critically through his famous designer glasses and replied that such a position was "Trotskyite," that the FSLN firmly rejected Trotskyism, and that true Leninists knew that revolution "cannot be exported." Here, in 1987, the dictator of a floundering Third World revolution seemed more interested in attacking Trotskyism than in frankly answering consequential questions. As for the domestic opposition, Ortega demurred from my argument that the Arias plan depended upon political reconciliation and democratization at home. Instead, he defended his unleashing of the *turbas divinas,* which he characterized as spontaneous outbursts of popular revolutionary enthusiasm. But everyone there knew that the *turbas* were carefully controlled shock troops of the State Security, bused from one place to another in government trucks to stage attacks on such institutions as the opposition newspaper *La Prensa.*

As a result of what I observed on the trip, I eventually became a firm supporter of *contra* aid. While congressional liberals were waging a campaign to cut off all such military aid, I had come to understand that it was only the threat of a fully capable *contra* army that made the Sandinista leaders even contemplate any internal loosening up. Ortega, I thought, had received so many adoring delegations that he was counting on American liberals to tolerate and even welcome a left-wing dictatorship such as his own, and he believed he could be candid about its character. Indeed, not only hard leftists but also Democratic liberals favored his regime on the ground that it was immoral to intervene in Nicaragua's internal affairs. I was not surprised, when I talked to Lino Hernandez, courageous head of the country's Independent Permanent Commission on Human Rights, to find that he almost never received visits from congressional Democrats; all of his visitors from the U.S. were Republicans.

Returning to the United States, I wrote my first piece in favor of extending U.S. support to the *contra* military effort, published in the *Los Angeles Times*. I argued that with the Arias peace plan at stake, Congress should vote on behalf of continued *contra* military aid. In view of Sandinista admissions that they would never turn over power even if they lost an election, their continued calling out of the *turbas,* and the arrest of major civic opponents of the regime, for me the situation was now clear: "The passage of some form of *contra* aid—primarily humanitarian, with lethal aid held in escrow for a brief period—is actually a precondition for the type of negotiated solution favored by Arias." What all Americans, including the Left, should favor was an insistence that the demands of simple Nicaraguans for freedom not be put on the back burner. What the Sandinistas favored was an end to *contra* funding without any move toward democratization. Then they would use the demise of the *contra* offensive to consolidate power, crush the opposition and cement their ties with the Soviets.

As Penn Kemble had predicted a couple of years earlier, I had indeed come full circle. The force of events and the realization that the so-called left-wing regimes were disastrous developments for the peoples of the region had finally turned me around. What the Left ignored was that while the Sandinistas' internal structure had become more repressive, the *contras* had managed to purge their own torturers and extremists, and had instituted a measure of internal reform that quickly made them into an autonomous and popular insurgency that was slowly winning peasant support in the rural areas of Nicaragua. The Sandinistas made one major error: they believed their own propaganda that the people supported them, and that they could afford to agree to an election since it was inevitable that they would win hands down.

Independent commentators, like my anti-Sandinista friend Bob Leiken, predicted in op-eds that it was quite likely the Sandinistas would lose the election on February 25, 1990; but few believed him. On the eve of the election, the papers were filled with predictions of a major Sandinista victory, one that would establish them firmly as the legitimate rulers of Nicaragua, this time with a democratic mandate. As the world learned, Nicaraguans told Western pollsters one thing, but voted otherwise, because the monitors from all over the world (including Jimmy Carter) enabled them to vote their conscience without fear.

I was there to witness the final outcome. Once again, I accompanied Nina Shea on a mission organized by the Puebla Institute to join in monitoring the voting in different regions. Actually, the Sandinista government had made us *personae non gratae*. They refused to give Shea and me visas for travel, or to give Puebla the status of legitimate observers. Nina and I decided to try going anyway.

Arriving in Managua, we found so much activity and commotion at the airport that Sandinista customs officers were in peak, inefficient operating status. When we got to the passport and visa control booth, we merely passed through without anyone asking for documents. As we approached the credentials office handing out government credentials to registered international monitors, our luck ran out. We were not on their list, we were told, and we would not be given documents. This meant we could not gain free access to monitor polling stations and conduct interviews. As I glanced at the credentials of other monitors, I came up with an easy solution. The document was apparently nothing more than a simple card with the investigator's photo attached, duly laminated and with a small stamp of the Sandinista government on the back. It was about the size of an American driver's license. I proposed to Nina that we enter as if we were credentialed, and if asked, flash our driver's licenses. It worked.

Managua was more like it had been in 1983 than my second visit in 1987. The Inter-Continental was once again packed. This time, though, it was impossible to get a room, so Nina and I shared a house rented from wealthy Nicaraguans by Jim Denton, then with the National Forum Foundation, and journalist P. J. O'Rourke, who was covering the election for *Rolling Stone*. But our focus each day was the Inter-Continental, where everybody who was anybody would be. I immediately spotted the leading Hollywood leftist and Sandinista supporter, Ed Asner, then a major television star who helped lead the anti-interventionist movement. I decided to approach him and introduce myself. As a result of *The Rosenberg File*, Asner had publicly blamed me for the failure of the movie based on E. L. Doctorow's novel *The Book of Daniel*, a *roman à clef* about the Rosenbergs. I was surprised when he quickly embraced me and said, "Ron Radosh, so glad to finally meet you." He could afford to be magnanimous, I guess. Like others, he was there to witness what he expected would be cause for celebration. I tried to caution him that it might not go his way, but he appeared confident.

The morning of the election, we drove at 5 A.M. way out into the countryside. Throughout the day, we observed scores of different polls, interviewed those waiting in line, and watched to see if ballots were being doctored. The few times we were asked for official credentials, we showed our driver's licenses. Since most of the poll watchers did not read English, they looked at our photos, assumed we were legitimate, and let us in. It was apparent early on that the Sandinistas would lose by a large majority. We picked up Sandinista soldiers, supposedly the most loyal to the government, and gave them rides from their bases to the polling station. Their conversations, indicating that they too would be voting for the opposition candidate Violeta Chamorro, widow of the famous *La Prensa* editor Pedro Joaquin, convinced us that the Sandinista victory predicted by U.S. pollsters was an illusion.

Late in the evening, everyone gathered at the Inter-Continental to await results. At 9 P.M., the U.N. observers' quick count of less than 10 percent of the vote showed Chamorro way ahead. An hour later, it was clear to the senior Sandinista leaders that they were facing a total disaster. Word filtered down quickly to the pack of journalists, fellow travelers of the Sandinistas and others waiting at the crowded outdoor pool and bar area of the hotel. As the first returns were broadcast, total silence descended upon the shocked journalists. Bianca Jagger, back again—this time ready to film a movie that would depict their anticipated electoral victory—was sobbing loudly as it became apparent that her beloved Sandinistas were not going to win. Around all the other tables were the glum faces of journalists there to celebrate a slap in the face to America, and unable to comprehend what had happened. At our table, Nina and I and others clapped and cheered as we heard each area's returns showing Violeta Chamorro's lead increasing. As expected, we received glares and scornful looks. At first, the Sandinista leaders were nowhere to be seen or heard from. Jimmy Carter was frantically trying to get to Daniel Ortega, but the president would not return his calls. Finally, just before midnight, Carter heard from him. By 2 A.M., after long negotiations, Ortega agreed to let the complete vote be released, and the nation knew that the revolutionary era had come to an end. At 6 o'clock the following morning he came on camera and conceded defeat to Violeta Chamorro. She had won by a total of 55 percent to Ortega's 41 percent.

Nina and I returned to the airport after a night of parties and receptions, where members of the opposition sang and drank and cheered their good fortune. I saw Alfonso Robelo, once a member of the first Sandinista government, and later a *contra* leader in exile, now circulating freely, ready again to take part in his business community. At the airport, it seemed that all security had come to a halt. Luggage was taken aboard aircraft without inspection, and the security machines were not operative. But as Nina and I were presenting our passports and tickets to move onto the plane, we were abruptly stopped. Checking his list, the Sandinista guard said that our name was not on any list, and we had no permission to enter the country. This, of course, was true, but I pointed out to him that since we had in fact entered, and since they had lost the election, it made no sense to prevent us from leaving. He didn't listen. Instead, he took us into separate rooms and told us to wait. "You must stay in Nicaragua," he said. An hour later, we were finally allowed to board the plane. I was tense until we hit the tarmac in Miami.

Months afterward, I attended a session in New York at the Council on Foreign Relations, where Alejandro Bendana, the young and charismatic spokesman for Daniel Ortega, was speaking. Bendana had attended Harvard University, where he had been the roommate of James LeMoyne, who had replaced Stephen Kinzer as the Central America correspondent for the *New York Times*. Bendana was best known as the man who appeared regularly on ABC's *Nightline,* suavely representing the Sandinista regime and cause. After his speech, I asked what had happened. "We messed up," he said. "I had given the orders that you and Shea not be allowed into the country, and somehow you got in. I guess our great security apparatus wasn't up to par." There was a silence. Then he spoke again: "I just don't understand what happened to you. You used to be on our side."

Bendana would a few years later write a well-circulated, self-critical article in which he acknowledged the growing strength of the *contras* among the people at the end of the Sandinista reign. And it would be revealed that all the time he was Ortega's chief spokesman and married to Ortega's stepdaughter, Bendana was fully aware that the Sandinista president was molesting his wife, and had regularly raped her since her pre-teens. That revelation, coming as it did in the waning years of the twentieth century, was perhaps an epitaph on charismatic Communists and the movements they made.

Upon returning home, I wrote a long essay for New York *Newsday,* one of the large-circulation city tabloids. Headlined "The U.S. Left Wasn't Right in Nicaragua" and appearing a week after the Chamorro victory, the piece was also my own goodbye to Nicaragua and to the broader American Left that had supported the Sandinista revolution. Going through the Left's tortured history of support for Third World dictators, I wrote: "At each turn of events, the liberal-left community in the United States looked the other way." They had always looked the other way. The only law the Left obeyed was Don't Look Back—for if it did, the only accomplishments it would see were famine, gulags and mass death.

The Nicaraguan election ended the prospects for revolution in Central America. It also ended my own long exile from America.

12

Coming Home

By 1990, New York City was becoming a rough place to live. Allis couldn't stand it, and constantly argued that we should consider moving. Once David Dinkins became mayor, the city grew markedly worse. The traffic island in the middle of Broadway, across from our apartment on West Ninety-third Street, began to resemble a 1930s Hooverville. Mentally disturbed individuals, let out from institutions and with no place to go, began to set up tents and live on the traffic islands. Walking our son, Michael, to public school, we were often accosted by bums—or the unfortunate homeless, as some of my friends called them—who would grab us and demand money.

My remaining liberal friends argued that the epidemic of homelessness was caused by Reaganism, and studiously avoided dealing with the implications of the liberal policies of deinstitutionalizing the mentally ill and rewarding people for not working, which had helped cause the crisis. The newspapers spilled a lot of ink on the so-called "Wild Man of Ninety-sixth Street," a mentally disturbed man not far from us who always returned to the street after a brief commitment, and who went about defacing cars (including our new Chrysler) with a pen knife. After he pushed a young schoolgirl in front of a moving car and almost killed her, he was sent away—at least for a little while.

In Michael's school, the much-publicized model school PS 87—supposedly the best elementary school not just in the city, but in the nation—one of the teachers known to the kids as "Mr. Malcolm" never changed his clothes, smelled to high heaven, and could hardly speak coherently, let alone teach anything. Sol Stern, whose son also attended the school and was a grade behind Mike, launched a campaign to get him fired. I joined in the effort, and called the president of the United Federation of Teachers, Sandy Feldman, a social democrat who had started her political life in the Young People's Socialist League as a follower of Max Shachtman. Sandy blamed the man's presence at the school on the principal, who would not fire him. When I spoke to the principal, she explained that union regulations made it virtually impossible to remove him, and that indeed, he had over the years been passed from school to school with good recommendations. He had seniority and had never had any charges brought against him, so her hands were tied. Finally, Sol threatened to call the TV news people to film the teacher in the schoolyard, as children moved away from him in disgust. The board of education didn't want that kind of publicity in the very school where the new assistant chancellor was sending his own children, so finally "Mr. Malcolm" was moved out—to a desk job where he maintained his full salary as a teacher but had no contact with children.

While all this was happening, I was getting fed up with conditions at the City University. The New York City Board of Higher Education was determined to deal with problems at the university by increasing the teaching load. At regular universities, most professors had a nine-credit load and taught different courses in their own specialties. Our condition was more like a factory: we taught the same sections of basic Western Civilization courses over and over. When the mandate came through that our load was to be increased from twelve to fifteen hours a week, or five courses per semester, I knew the time had come to get out.

At that exact moment, I luckily got a phone call from Al Shanker, president of the American Federation of Teachers, whom I had met recently at a dinner. An ally of AFL-CIO chief Lane Kirkland, Shanker was a fierce anti-Communist. He had started out like his protégé Sandy Feldman in the old Socialist Party, and had begun to organize teachers into what was originally a small Socialist-led union, created to counter the Communist-led Teachers' Union that dominated the New York school system in the 1940s. Shanker came to prominence when he led a strike against the system, closing down the city's schools and going to jail until the demand for union recognition was won. And in the 1960s, Shanker received more attention when black militants in Ocean Hill–Brownsville, in a naked coup rationalized by a new system of "local control," illegally fired white Jewish teachers in order to replace them with black instructors. Shanker responded again by calling a citywide strike. His position as head of the UFT made him the most powerful teachers' union leader in the nation, and eventually he won the presidency of the national AFL-CIO-affiliated teachers' union.

In 1992, Shanker asked me if I would consider coming to Washington, D.C., to work as his executive assistant. It happened that the City University had just announced an "early retirement" package to induce faculty to leave the system earlier than they had planned. Shanker said the job he envisioned for me would allow me to plan strategy, travel with him through the country and to Europe, help him write articles and speeches, and generally operate as a brain trust for the union. Al was an unorthodox and principled man, an advocate of school reform, a supporter of charter schools, and a man who often took positions his own membership disagreed with. I jumped at the opportunity to become part of his iconoclasm and get out of a higher education system that was rapidly becoming infected with political correctness and deconstructionist dada. After a short trial run, I told Al I would sign on. Within two weeks, we bought a house in suburban Maryland and moved there before Michael's school term began.

As it turned out, Al Shanker's hope that I could play an important role in his organization was naïve. Instead of thinking and writing, I found myself stuck in a typical union bureaucracy, mired in make-work and acting as Shanker's intellectual gopher. During my time at the union, there were only two things I can say I was proud of—and both came to naught.

First, during the transition to the new Clinton administration, Al asked me to prepare a memo to the new president, which would be signed and sent in Al's name, regarding the National Endowment for the Humanities. I wrote a long proposal urging Bill Clinton to appoint an NEH chairman who would be opposed to political correctness and be pledged to standards of academic excellence. I presented a list of prominent individuals who could fit the bill, including people like Shelby Steele and John H. Bunzel. The subsequent history of that organization under the new Clinton administration is evidence enough of our memo's ultimate impact.

The second task I took some pride in also pertained to the issue of political correctness. Al Shanker had a weekly column that the AFT bought space for in journals and newspapers, called "Where We Stand." He had hired a regular writer who would talk over with Al what he wanted to say and then write the column. A few times, when a special issue came up that he knew I was interested in, he asked me to write it. Finally, Al came to me and said it was time we made a statement on the intellectual and moral decline of the universities. I wrote a tough editorial, which Al read and gave his OK before going off to Europe. In his absence, his top aide at the AFT spiked the column. "My job is to protect Al from himself," she told me.

I also got in some trouble when the controversy erupted over Clinton's scheduled—but never announced—appointment of Johnetta Cole to the position of secretary of education. Cole was an African-American educator and college president whom I knew to have been an unabashed Communist fellow traveler. And, as a major news story in the Jewish paper *The Forward* showed, she also had been a leader of the Venceremos Brigades, and sat on the executive board of the U.S. Peace Council, the American affiliate of the Soviet-created World Peace Council, for whom she had signed a statement accusing the United States of displaying a "history of aggression and genocidal practices against people of color around the world."

My late friend Eric Breindel, writing in the *New York Post*, said that if Cole got that appointment, it would send an "inescapable" message that the new administration was "not interested in distinguishing between a Left-liberal and someone who cast her lot with the cause of Communist totalitarianism." One of her most outspoken defenders was Jesse Jackson, who argued that "Jewish complaints" were hurting her chances for a Cabinet appointment. Al Shanker, of course, was a committed anti-Communist, and so he was aghast at Cole's impending appointment to such a high post. The concern of others in the AFT, however, was that the incoming Clinton administration, which they strongly supported and had campaigned for, would be hurt by open criticism. Rather than condemn Cole's unsavory background after it was exposed by journalist David Twersky in *The Forward,* they only cared about doing damage control for Clinton. I was called into the office of some of the AFT's senior executives. "We know you wrote that article in *The Forward,*" said the political director, Rachelle Horowitz. "You have to understand that at the AFT, anything you write reflects on us, and that you're not free to do work under your own name that will hurt us." I protested that I had not written the article at issue, and pointed out that any reporter worth his salt could easily have found the information about Cole in the public record. It was true that Twersky, Robert Novak and other reporters had phoned me, since they were all aware I would have known of Cole, and they wanted confirmation of her hard-left politics. But nothing I said could convince my skeptical AFT colleagues that I had not written the article that broke the story. Horowitz kept reiterating, "We know it was you." Clearly, my AFT career was not meant to be.

I left the AFT in June 1993. For six months I worked for the United States Information Agency, researching and writing a report on Radio and TV Marti commissioned by Congress before it voted on what to do about the propaganda service beamed into Cuba. I was amazed to find that I easily received a security clearance to examine classified material and to have CIA and State Department briefings; evidently, my radical past had disappeared down some memory hole. After this job was over, I became an Olin Professor of History at Adelphi University, and for two years I commuted back to New York each week to teach in their new Honors Division. When Adelphi became consumed by internal problems, I looked for other teaching positions. Although I had a good résumé and record of publication, I found that I was now a pariah in the world of academe. I applied for a job in the history department at George Washington University, where, if I had still been a Communist writing left-wing history, I probably would have breezed in. But faculty members practicing a politically correct version of McCarthyism blackballed me. Eventually I obtained a nonteaching position at the GWU Center for Communitarian Policy Studies as a result of a kind invitation from its director, Amitai Etzioni, and the university's president, Stephen Trachtenberg.

Much had been lost in my life, but more had been gained. The move to Washington, D.C., gave me new friends and an atmosphere quite different from the charged, left-wing world of the Upper West Side of Manhattan; it allowed me to sit back and think things over. I felt intellectually liberated, and began moving in new directions. In an essay about intellectuals and the Spanish Civil War written for Hilton Kramer's journal, the *New Criterion,* I concluded that the Spanish Republic, for which so many left-wing intellectuals and activists (including my own uncle) had fought in the 1930s, had been turned into a totalitarian police state by Moscow and the Spanish Communists, and would have become a People's Republic had it survived. Life under the commissars would have been a worse fate than life under Franco. This article, by desecrating the last sacred ground of the Left, provoked a storm. When Irving Howe answered it scathingly in the pages of *Dissent,* it was clear that his concern was not Spain in the past, but rather the kindred causes of the contemporary Left, specifically apartheid in South Africa. Black liberation there, he wrote, had to be "our cause," even if it led "to Communist domination."

Howe's comments were an indicator of what had happened to the American Left in the era of Ronald Reagan. The same independent intellectual who once had tried to explain to the New Left that "it never was necessary to defend the Communist regime in Hanoi or the Vietcong guerrillas in order to oppose American intervention" was now, in the late 1980s, arguing against himself, asserting that the Left had to stand together with a group like the African National Congress even if this led to Communist control. The only question the Left now asked, as it had fifty years earlier, was "Which Side Are You On?"

The presence of my name on the editorial board of *Dissent* magazine was clearly an annoyance to Howe. I would have long since asked that it be removed, if Paul Berman, Manny Geltman and others involved with the journal had not been trying to expel me because of my views on Central America. (Geltman mailed me a letter in which he said, "whatever you are, you're not one of us.") I decided not to make it easy for them, so every time some innuendo came out about my not fitting in because of incorrect views, I said that I would leave the editorial board when they asked Marty Peretz to leave also. The publisher of the *New Republic* and at the time more conservative than I was, Marty had never attended a single *Dissent* editorial board meeting. But he was an old friend of Howe's, and especially of Michael Walzer's, the journal's coeditor and his onetime Brandeis University schoolmate. Moreover, Marty gave the magazine several thousand dollars a year, which made up for his decidedly nonsocialist political views. With Marty Peretz still on board, I refused to budge, out of sheer orneriness. But finally in 1995, as *Divided They Fell*, my history of the post-Vietnam Democratic Party, was about to be published, I wrote Walzer to say I no longer wanted to be associated with *Dissent*. He didn't bother to answer. But in the next issue of the magazine, I noticed that my name had been taken off the masthead. "I'll be lonely without you," Marty joked the next time I spoke to him.

By this time I was reading the work of earlier defectors from the Left, and was particularly struck by Sidney Hook's powerful autobiography, *Out of Step*. For many years, Hook had been intellectually and politically anathema to me. (Indeed, for a time, Hook was my parents' next-door neighbor, and I always adamantly refused to meet him.) Now, reading his fine book, I realized that he had gone through an experience quite similar to mine decades earlier—at a time when the totalitarians of the Left held major positions of influence in the cultural and political life of the nation, and standing apart from them meant being subjected to bitter calumnies. Hook defined the struggle for democracy as the need to stand against the totalitarianism of the Left and of the Right. Despite all of its "failings, drawbacks and limitations," he wrote, "the defense and survival of the West was the first priority." As I read these words in the 1990s, I had what Edmund Wilson once called "the shock of recognition," and my eyes filled with tears.

It has now been a little over a decade since the collapse of the Soviet Union, and of the Old Left it embodied—the Left that was my birthright. It has been three decades since the New Left, the Left of my youth, flamed out in histrionics and bloody fantasies of "revolutionary violence." And the leftover Left, that collection of postures and grievances, is still with us, and probably always will be—even though its history, as Francis Fukayama might say, has already effectively ended.

In its many shape-shifting forms—radical feminism, ultra-environmentalism, pro-Arabism, political correctness, the new anarchism—this leftover Left has developed new issues and causes, all fought for with the same earnestness, arrogance and thoughtlessness that we brought to the fight for communism and then socialism from the 1940s through the 1980s. Our history should have been a cautionary tale, but as the causes of yesteryear collapsed, my old friends found it hard to reevaluate their experiences or acknowledge that they were wrong. Instead, they repeated the platitudes about "real" socialism never having been tried, and about "actually existing socialism" having been tried first in the wrong country. Today's Left has no Soviet Union as a beacon, but its reflexive hatred of the American system is intact, and its devotees have no qualms about running off to join with the young, self-proclaimed "anarchists" who trash Starbucks and picket the World Bank and the International Monetary Fund, the institutions that for them symbolize the abiding evil of big corporations and international capitalism.

I watch the unfolding of events with profound thankfulness that the stakes are lower now than when the New Left of the 1960s sought to demolish America from within. I am aware that the capacity for harm is diminished because so many stood solidly behind America while we tried to bring it down. The country is stronger for having encountered and withstood us.

As we enter the twenty-first century, my own life has come full circle. I spent the first presidential election of the new century in China, where I had the task of traveling throughout the last major communist nation to explain the nature of the American democratic system and delineate the issues dividing George W. Bush and Al Gore. Everywhere I went in China, I spoke before large and enthusiastic audiences, all of them friendly to the United States, anxious to learn about our political democracy, and fascinated with the notion that citizens could actually choose their nation's top leader. Sponsored by the office of public diplomacy in the State Department, I stood before Chinese university students and intellectuals as a proud representative of the United States. And with a keen appreciation of the irony involved, I was the first American citizen allowed to speak to China's "cadres-in-training," as an embassy diplomat called them, at the official Central Party School in Beijing, run by the Chinese Communist Party. A former Communist explaining the merits of America's democratic political system to the cream of the remnant of true believers in Communist China: what a concept!

I don't see much of my old comrades these days. But I know that some of them continue to dream secretly of revolution, and still refuse to prepare a profit-and-loss statement on their past commitments. Arthur Koestler defined them once and for all when he wrote that "clinging to the last shred of the torn illusion is typical of the intellectual cowardice that prevails on the left." I once thought it would be impossible to live without these illusions; now I know that I would never have become a free man if I hadn't managed to get rid of them on my long journey home.

Acknowledgments

I WOULD NOT HAVE WRITTEN THIS BOOK WITHOUT THE ENCOUR-
agement and suggestions of Peter Collier and David Horowitz.
Both of them thought that my life and experiences on the left
would be a story of interest to others, and that I should take the
plunge and write it. I hope their enthusiasm turns out to be
warranted.

Peter Collier is not only a good friend, but also my editor.
Others told me to expect the best, and they were right. Peter is
the opposite of many editors at major publishing houses, where
authors often find that their books go essentially unedited, with
only perfunctory attention paid to them. By contrast, Peter
devoted an inordinate amount of time to my manuscript. He cut
mercilessly, and saved me from unwieldy sentences and purple
prose. For this I am forever in his debt.

Through the years, I have weathered the storm with the support of loyal friends. High on that list are Louis Menashe and his
wife, Sheila. Though we disagree about much, Louis has discussed my political views endlessly and has bravely backed my
right to change my mind, still maintaining his friendship while
others became ex-friends. I also value the friendship and support of Fred Siegel, who himself has changed his views as I have
revised mine. My dear friend Danny Kalb, a guitarist's guitarist,
has engaged me in many discussions of our convergent paths.
And on the political left, my friendship with Jesse Lemisch has
somehow managed to survive what to him must be an inexpli-
cable apostasy. In Washington, D.C., and Atlanta, Georgia, I have
shared a community of interest, friendship and scholarship with

my friends John E. Haynes and Harvey Klehr. I thank them for everything.

I have dedicated this book to my wife, Allis. She has read the manuscript, made numerous suggestions, and saved me from many errors. And for the past twenty-five years, she has lived with me the experiences related here. I would not have written the book or reached my present stage without her devotion and love.

Index